A HOME AWAY FROM HOME

True Stories of Wild Animal Sanctuaries

NICHOLAS READ

*To Carolyn, Peter, Scott,
and Paul for helping me
through some very tough
times. Thank you all.*

Heritage House Publishing Company Ltd.
heritagehouse.ca

Cataloguing information available from Library and Archives Canada
978-1-77203-219-2 (pbk)
978-1-77203-212-3 (ebook)

Edited by Sarah Harvey
Cover and interior book design by Setareh Ashrafologhalai
Cover photographs from The Elephant Sanctuary in Tennessee (top)
and Chimp Haven (bottom).

The interior of this book was produced on FSC®-certified, acid-
free paper, processed chlorine free and printed with vegetable-
based inks.

Heritage House gratefully acknowledges that the land on which we
live and work is within the traditional territories of the Lkwungen
(Esquimalt and Songhees), Malahat, Pacheedaht, Scia'new, T'Sou-ke,
and W̱SÁNEĆ (Pauquachin, Tsartlip, Tsawout, Tseycum) Peoples.

We acknowledge the financial support of the Government of Canada
through the Canada Book Fund (CBF) and the Canada Council for
the Arts, and the Province of British Columbia through the British
Columbia Arts Council and the Book Publishing Tax Credit.

24 23 22 21 20   1 2 3 4 5

Printed in Canada

CONTENTS

Wildlife Rescue & Rehabilitation (WRR) is one of the oldest and largest wildlife sanctuaries in the United States. WRR's spacious, open-top, natural enclosures are unique and tailored for each resident species.
WILDLIFE RESCUE & REHABILITATION, INC.

AUTHOR'S NOTE

THEY SAY the only constant is change. That's true of animal sanctuaries too. As you'll read in this book, sanctuaries are no longer just for dogs, cats, and horses. Other animals—ones you would never associate with North America—have to rely on them too. For years, wild and often exotic animals have been pulled out of their natural homes to be put on display in North American zoos. More than that, some of them have ended up as pets. While the idea of keeping a lion, a monkey, or a python as a companion animal may seem crazy to you, it's not to other people. More people than you would expect. The trouble is that, far too often, such people have no idea how to look after these animals properly, so it's left to sanctuaries to rescue them and care for them instead.

It's unfortunate that we have so little respect for nature that we've come to regard a creature as regal as a tiger as a pet. Something to show off on the end of a leash. But that's what things have come to in parts of the Canada and the US. This is why sanctuaries for these animals are so important. It's the rare individual who has the courage and the money to set up a home for unwanted and often abused elephants, leopards, and chimpanzees, but happily, such marvellous, selfless people do exist. You will read about some of them in this book, and how they are devoting their lives to animals who, without them, would have no other place to go.

You'll also find out how you can help these people and the animals they look after. As you can imagine, creating and maintaining a good home for big cats, big snakes, and big birds—mainly parrots—is no easy endeavour. It's practically miraculous. If the animals could, they would say "thank you" many, many times, because they literally owe these sanctuaries their lives.

NICHOLAS READ

INTRODUCTION
OUT OF PLACE

HANNAH IS a hippo. A 226-kilogram (500-pound) pygmy hippo with gunmetal grey skin, a body like a barrel, and teeth the size of two-scoop ice cream cones. Pygmy hippos live in the forests and swamps of West Africa—mainly Liberia—where they spend most of their time eating grass, leaves, and fruit, and bathing in rivers. But Hannah lives at the Fund for Animals Wildlife Center in Ramona, California. In fact, she's never set foot in Africa. Her whole life has been lived in the United States, going from home to home to home.

Hannah was born in 1973 at the National Zoo in Washington, DC, which makes her the oldest pygmy hippo in North America. When she was grown, she was sent to the Austin Zoo in Texas, where zookeepers hoped she would become a mother. When she didn't, she was moved to the San Diego Zoo and Safari Park in California, but she didn't stay long because she didn't like the other hippos there. That's not surprising as pygmy hippos tend to be solitary creatures. So in 1994 she was transferred again to the home of a private exotic animal keeper. His place wasn't a zoo or a sanctuary, and he wasn't a zookeeper or a biologist. He was just a guy who liked keeping rare animals. If that surprises you, it shouldn't. People all over Canada and the US keep wild animals in apartments, condos, and suburban backyards. In fact, Hannah's keeper already had another hippo when he got Hannah.

What a sad fate for the queen of the jungle. She should be taking down gazelles on the African savannah. Instead she's handed scraps of food in this decrepit roadside zoo. HUMANE SOCIETY OF THE UNITED STATES

Trouble was, Hannah didn't like that hippo either, so off she went to yet another keeper who agreed to house her by herself. That might have suited her, except her new keeper didn't have the facilities to look after her properly. There was no swimming pool, no shade, and no mud, which pygmy hippos love to roll in. So Hannah was miserable. She was in rough shape, too. When she was finally rescued by the Fund for Animals Wildlife Center in 2002, she had a second-degree sunburn and a skin infection.

She's fine now. At the time this book was written she was 45—old for a hippo—but happy. She lives in a sanctuary where all her needs are met. She has a 1,200 square-metre (13,000 square-foot) paddock—about a quarter the size of a soccer pitch—and in the paddock is a heated shelter. There's also a concrete swimming pool, and a natural pond with muddy banks for Hannah to roll in. In the pool is a giant soccer ball that she knocks about like a midfielder, and a big drum that she treats like a raft. She's very protective of her pond and drives away any bird or animal foolish enough to venture into it—with one exception. For a while, a pair of mallard ducks (and their babies) wandered into the pool any time they wished. She even let them nibble from her food bowl. No one knows why.

Hannah shares the sanctuary with eleven other permanent residents: nine bobcats, a coyote, and a cougar. She can only see two of the bobcats from her enclosure, and because she's nocturnal, she only sees them at night. All the other animals at the sanctuary are there temporarily. They are wild animals native to California who come in with injuries or illnesses, are restored to health, and then returned to nature.

But all over the US and Canada there are sanctuaries where exotic animals like Hannah—great apes, monkeys, elephants, birds, reptiles, and big cats—live out their whole lives in the care of humans who have established places for them where they are loved and looked after according to their own particular needs. The original meaning of the word *sanctuary* is a place of holiness and safety, which is exactly what modern-day animal sanctuaries are.

This book is about these sanctuaries. It is about places where animals, many of whom were never meant to be in North America, spend their lives in as much comfort as the people who run the sanctuaries can provide. It is about places where elephants can be elephants, tigers can be tigers, and chimpanzees can be chimpanzees. Sanctuaries can never hope to be a substitute for the wild—they are too small and artificial—but they are the next best thing. And for animals who were brought here as captives, sanctuaries can be the difference between life and death.

This cougar should be roaming the woods of North America, not cooped up in a jail. HUMANE SOCIETY OF THE UNITED STATES

THE HISTORY OF ANIMAL SANCTUARIES

How did we reach this bizarre and unnatural state? For an answer, we have to go back to 1828, the year the world's first zoo opened in London, England. Curiously, it took almost half a century for the notion of a zoo to catch on in North America—it wasn't until 1874 that Philadelphia opened America's first zoo—but once the idea caught on, it was unstoppable. New York caught up to Philadelphia a few years later. Then Chicago, Washington, and Boston. Canada's first zoo, Toronto's Riverdale Zoo, opened in 1887. Vancouver's Stanley Park Zoo followed in 1888. Soon every

This tiger was never meant to be in North America. But he's lucky. He's now living the best life he can outside the wild at the Performing Animal Welfare Society sanctuary in California. PAWS

city of any size had one. Today there are 230 in the US officially recognized, or accredited, by the Association of Zoos and Aquariums (AZA) and 27 in Canada accredited by the Canadian Association of Zoos and Aquariums. There are other zoos too, but no one knows how many because they aren't accredited.

But as more and more zoos opened, a curious character began to appear alongside them: the exotic-animal keeper. For these people, seeing exotic animals wasn't enough. They wanted to own them too. And thanks to zoos, it wasn't long before they could. That's because zoos of the day bred too many babies. People loved looking at baby animals—they still do—so zoos bred them deliberately. A new bear or lion cub could mean thousands of extra visitors coming through the zoo's gates, which meant significantly higher earnings for

the zoo. But these babies had an annoying way of growing up. And when they did, there wasn't room to keep them—an adult animal requires a good deal more space than a baby—so they had to be gotten rid of. Enter the exotic-animal keeper. Many zoos didn't care that these keepers didn't have the facilities to look after the animals properly; all that mattered was that the animals were gone.

Today, no one knows how many zoo animals are sold to exotic-animal dealers. In 1999, the *San Jose Mercury News* published an exposé that said one third of all surplus animals born in zoos were hauled away to exotic-animal keepers. But that was over 20 years ago, and things have improved since then. Zoos are watched more closely, so they're not as cavalier about getting rid of extra lions, camels, and bears as they once were.

That's not to say they don't. But the numbers are smaller. Some still go to dilapidated roadside zoos. Some end up in circuses and cheap travelling shows of the kind you find in rundown malls. "Come and pet the tiger"—that sort of thing. And yes, some continue to go to exotic-animal dealers. Then it's anyone's guess where they end up. In basements, tool sheds, garages? Who knows?

But some—the lucky few like Hannah— end up in sanctuaries run by people who give their lives, their bank accounts, and their properties to looking after animals who were never meant to set foot out of Africa, Asia, or South America. Because humans captured and transported their parents or grandparents to the US or Canada, they have to be looked after in conditions created by people. Instead of chasing gazelles, captive lions push tire swings. Captive chimpanzees play with dolls. Hannah knocks around that soccer ball.

THE TRADE IN EXOTIC ANIMALS

Today, the main source of animals in exotic-animal sanctuaries is the legal and illegal trade in exotic pets, which is almost as rich as the drug trade. Tens of thousands of exotic animals are born in captivity each year in North America—many more tigers are born in Canada and the US than will ever live in India—while thousands of wild birds and reptiles are still caught in the jungles of Africa, Asia, and South America. Sanctuaries have to exist because people get rid of exotic animals as readily as they acquire them. In fact, the exotic-animal trade is so ravenous that there will never be enough sanctuaries to accommodate all the animals who need them.

How do people acquire an exotic pet? It's easier than you think. Pet shops routinely sell reptiles, amphibians, and birds. And until recently, you could find them in a printed monthly magazine called the *Animal Finders Guide*. One edition listed Bactrian and dromedary camels, Aldabra tortoises (a giant tortoise species native to the Seychelles Islands), Siberian lynx kittens, wolf pups, emus, and even a two-year-old yak.

Now that computers have taken the place of print, you have to look online. Google almost any kind of animal and you'll probably see an online ad for it. Some of these ads are scams. The sellers will dupe buyers into sending them money for a chimp, an elephant, or a tiger without any intention of sending an animal in return. But other ads are real. Search "giraffe for sale" and up pops one website with an offer of a female baby giraffe for—get this—$60,000! You can also find an albino wallaby (with white fur instead of brown) and a Grant's zebra in the range of $3,000. A second site will sell you a Morelet's crocodile (a rare freshwater crocodile native to Guatemala and Belize) for under $1,000, and on yet another site you can get a baby black-and-white lemur for more than $5,000.

But even the Internet isn't the unlimited source of exotic animals it once was. People have started to get wise to its scams, and newspapers and TV news programs have begun to expose this dubious trade.

Petting a tiger might seem like a cool idea, but it can be extremely dangerous and damaging for both people and tigers. Wild animals should never be kept as pets, for both their own sakes and the people around them. HUMANE SOCIETY OF THE UNITED STATES

Consequently, many sellers have taken down their ads and begun to rely on old-fashioned word-of-mouth. You probably don't know anyone with a lion to sell, but the owner of your nearest roadside zoo might. In other words, he just might know a man who knows a man with a king of the jungle to unload.

Is it any wonder that exotic animal sanctuaries have to exist? And once exotic animals are in them, they're in them for good. There's no sending them back to the countries they (or their ancestors) came from. Why? For one thing, there is less and less wilderness available for the world's truly wild creatures, let alone an army of exotic animals born and raised in captivity (as most exotic pets are). And for another, such animals couldn't survive the wild. They would starve to death or be killed by a genuinely wild neighbour, a trophy hunter, or a poacher. The only place left for these misfits is a sanctuary. No one knows for sure how many exotic animal sanctuaries there are in Canada and the US because no one keeps a list of them. But there are a lot—good ones, bad ones, and those in between.

This book is about the good ones, the animals who live in them, and the people who sacrifice everything to run them.

DURING THE 1990S, former world heavy-weight boxing champion Mike Tyson owned three white Bengal tigers—Kenya, Storm, and Boris—who reportedly cost him $210,000 to buy and $4,000 a month to take care of. But in 2003, Tyson went bankrupt and had to sell the tigers. Storm was bought by a tattoo artist in Indiana, who kept him and two other tigers in his tattoo shop until 2010, when the malnourished cats were taken by the US Department of Agriculture. Now Tyson is said to keep pigeons, but his fondness for big cats was recalled in the hit movie *The Hangover*, in which Tyson, playing himself, claims a tiger is stolen from his home.

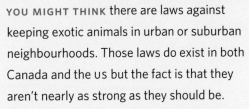

YOU MIGHT THINK there are laws against keeping exotic animals in urban or suburban neighbourhoods. Those laws do exist in both Canada and the US but the fact is that they aren't nearly as strong as they should be.

In the US, all but five states have some laws about the private possession of dangerous wild animals—like venomous snakes, lions, bears, and wolves. Yet it's still pretty easy to get your hands on them. The same is true in Canada. And if regulations do exist, they vary widely from province to province and state to state.

Even when laws are passed, they're rarely enforced. With the number of state and provincial conservation officers being cut all the time, there simply isn't the money or the will to make sure everyone's behaving themselves.

The Performing Animal Welfare Society sanctuary in northern California, with its green rolling hills and acres of grass, is a haven for exotic animals rescued from the entertainment and pet industries. PAWS

1

THE HIGH COST OF CARING

Wildlife Rescue & Rehabilitation is home to more than 300 animals commonly found on farms, including sheep, goats, cows, chickens, geese, ducks, donkeys, mules, and pigs. WILDLIFE RESCUE & REHABILITATION, INC.

A S A BOY, Ed Stewart was pretty much like everyone else when it came to animals. He liked them well enough, but he never gave them much thought. He once asked his dad about getting a dog, but the thought vanished like mist on a river when he learned how much responsibility they were.

He felt the same when he went to the University of Tennessee to study communications. Animals were like furniture: there to be petted if one was in the room but forgotten if they weren't. What he really longed for was adventure—and success.

After graduating in 1973, he worked in Florida and Ohio for a while, but it was California that beckoned. Stewart moved west, taking a job promoting Ford's Lincoln-Mercury line of cars. Ford no longer makes the Mercury, but at the time it was considered a desirable car. Something your dad moved up to when he got a new, better-paying job. Stewart would go to car shows around the country, showing off Mercury's latest line-up, which included a sporty model called the Cougar and a compact car called the Bobcat. Because of these cars, Mercury operated under "the sign of the cat," and Mercury commercials would end with an actual cougar sitting atop a Lincoln-Mercury sign, growling.

Two cougars did the growling back then, one named Chauncey and the other named Christopher. Both belonged to a passionate,

Believe it or not, back in the 1970s the Ford Motor Company used live cougars to advertise its cars, the Cougar and the Bobcat. PAWS

determined, and young animal trainer Pat Derby. Unlike Stewart, Derby, who died of cancer in 2013, loved animals. You might even say she lived for them. What she hated was the way Hollywood treated them. 40 years ago, animals were no better than props in movies—a lion roaring in a jungle, a dog barking in a lane, a bird chirping in a cage. Mere background to the principal action on the screen. And when their usefulness was done, so were they. How and where they were disposed of wasn't Hollywood's concern. Either someone

rescued them, or they died. Who knew? Who cared?

Derby did. And when she met Stewart, she made him care too. They were at a car show in Cleveland in 1976, and it was soulmates at first sight. Stewart was there with Lincoln-Mercury and Derby was there with Christopher. (Chauncey had since passed away.) Incredibly, live cougars were a staple at car shows of the time. It wasn't until one mauled a nine-year-old boy at a Pittsburgh show in 1982 that the practice ended. The cat, a

60-kilogram (130-pound) male named Tom-Tom, escaped his handler and pinned the boy by the throat. Luckily, an off-duty police officer used his gun to shoot Tom-Tom or the boy may have died.

But when Stewart met Derby, Lincoln-Mercury thought nothing of bringing live predators the size of racing bikes to events attended by thousands of people. And much as Derby hated exploiting Christopher that way, the fees she earned displaying him helped pay for the care of him and other animals in her keep.

It was also thanks to her and Christopher's presence at the show that she got to introduce Stewart to the Hollywood she knew and despised. She'd even written a book about it called *The Lady and the Tiger.* She showed him first-hand elephants shackled in chains and tigers penned in cages not much bigger than they were. At the beginning, Stewart just wanted to be with Derby, but what she showed him shocked him, too. Like Derby, he couldn't understand why other people weren't outraged as well. "I thought, my God, this is not even close to what I expected. The whole industry had a kind of false front on it. People think animals used in entertainment would be the most pampered, cared for, cherished animals in the world because they're in the enter-tainment business. But it was nothing like

This black bear, named Ben, should be living in the forests of Canada or the US, but because he was raised in captivity, he can't. He wouldn't know how to survive, so he instead lives at the Performing Animal Welfare Society sanctuary in California. PAWS

that. What I saw were small enclosures, ramshackle fences, and an abundance of animals in close quarters. It hit me imme-diately. There was something drastically wrong with this industry."

At the time, Derby had a property near Santa Barbara where she kept four bears, a tiger, and an elephant, in addition to Christopher. All of them had been rescued in one way or another from the enter-tainment industry. Shortly after, Stewart moved to the property too and, "through osmosis," learned how to look after the animals. It was the price he paid for being

Wildlife Rescue & Rehabilitation receives approximately 10,000 animals each year. The goal is to rehabilitate and release native wild animals and to provide sanctuary to non-releasable native and non-native wildlife. WILDLIFE RESCUE & REHABILITATION, INC.

with Derby, a woman he remembers as "a force of nature." "I had no intention of being in the industry," he says of his accidental initiation. "I didn't crave handling animals. I thought, 'this is crazy. This is dangerous.' We would walk a grizzly bear on a leash, and I thought this is crazy. But Pat thought it was normal. I thought it was crazy."

Crazy or not, it's how the two of them—and their menagerie—would live for the rest of their lives. They didn't know it at the time, but what Derby and Stewart were

beginning then was PAWS, the Performing Animal Welfare Society, the first sanctuary for large exotic animals in North America. Originally, PAWS was just a few fences on a patch of earth far too small for two people and seven large animals, but it now encompasses three properties and almost 1,000 hectares (2,500 acres) of ground in California. But small as it was, it was definitely a sanctuary in that the animals it housed were safe from harm and starvation. Their needs were always put first.

With so many large animals in their care, though, Derby and Stewart needed more land. So they used what little money they had to buy a 16-hectare (40-acre) property near Leggett in the California Redwoods, where they retired all their animals except Christopher, whose commercial appearances continued to help pay their bills. The property also had a restaurant, some holiday cabins to rent, and a gift shop, all intended to help the couple make money. And they did, but not enough. Never enough. "We took fatal blow after fatal blow," Stewart recalls. "But we always got up. I guess we were tough. Pat was the toughest person I've ever known. She was a fighter and didn't give up. I can't think of anybody who could have survived what we did."

In fact, not only did they survive, they managed, seven years later, to move to a new 12-hectare (30-acre) former

There aren't nearly as many captive lions as there are tigers in North America, but they're still here in zoos, in people's homes, and in sanctuaries like this one. PAWS

dog kennel and dairy farm near Galt in Sacramento County. Even though the property was smaller than the one they sold, it was more desirable because it was closer to Sacramento, the state capital, and Derby and Stewart wanted to be as close to Sacramento as they could. That's because in those days their priority wasn't running a sanctuary. It was creating an organization that would push for laws that would safeguard the welfare of all animals in entertainment, not just theirs.

Trouble was, people kept turning up with animals who needed a place to stay. The lion or tiger or bear in question was supposed to stay only for a night or two. But days had a way of turning into months, and months into years. After all, theirs was the only place of its kind in the state—actually, the whole country—where such animals could go. "It was never our plan to have a sanctuary," Stewart says. "We wanted to establish an organization where Pat could influence people and get laws and regulations passed. But what happened was that everybody, US Fish and Game, other animal groups, the [US Department of Agriculture], started asking us if we could take in animals. And Pat couldn't say no. How did we decide if we'd take in

▲ Wildlife Rescue & Rehabilitation (WRR) provides permanent sanctuary to non-releasable wildlife at its 212-acre sanctuary in Kendalia, Texas. WRR's spacious, open-top, natural enclosures are unique and tailored for each resident species. WILDLIFE RESCUE & REHABILITATION, INC.

➤ An infant bobcat kitten rescued by Wildlife Rescue & Rehabilitation after his mother was killed. WILDLIFE RESCUE & REHABILITATION, INC.

it's open to the public only four times a year, when supporters are invited—for a price and a carefully defined span of time—to meet the staff, enjoy some refreshments, and most importantly, view the animals.

TIME, MONEY, AND HEART

The 1980s were an important decade in the animal protection movement. For the first time, people spoke of animal rights, not just welfare, and organizations that championed those rights were established all over the US and Canada. Exotic animal sanctuaries like PAWS began to spring up too. Today many cities throughout Canada and the US may have one or even two sanctuaries that take in birds or reptiles. Sanctuaries for larger animals are rarer, but they exist too. According to Stewart, there could be as many as 1,200 in the US and Canada that house exotic animals. But only about 120 achieve any kind of lasting success. The rest, despite being established with the best of intentions, are teetering on a cliff.

an animal? I'd joke and say it depended on who answered the phone. The animals were always supposed to be temporary, but they never were. One lioness was supposed to stay for two days, and she stayed eleven years. A wolf was supposed to be there two days, and she lived to be seventeen."

So, in 1984, Derby and Stewart finally recognized the writing on the wall and established PAWS. They registered it as a charity within the state of California and opened their gates—and hearts—to animals who literally had nowhere else to turn. Today PAWS cares for more than 100 such animals—elephants, lions, tigers, bobcats, lynx, coyotes, cougars, and monkeys. And because PAWS is a sanctuary, a place where the animals come first,

The problem is that it practically takes a magician to run a good sanctuary. First, you have to find the right site. Then you have to build enclosures and things to climb and provide toys and medical facilities. Then you have to find the money not just to open the sanctuary, but to keep it going. If a sanctuary has to close, there may not be another sanctuary willing to take its animals. What would happen to them? The need for sanctuary space is always greater than its availability.

Lynn Cuny, who founded the Wildlife Rescue & Rehabilitation in Texas in 1977, puts it this way: "A big heart's lovely, but it's simply not enough." She's seen dozens of sanctuaries come and go, so she's well acquainted with what can, and often does, go wrong. "Good intentions are wonderful, but they're not enough when you have the lives of other sentient beings in your hands," she says. "There's nothing slight or minor or trivial about this work. You have got to be up for it, because it takes nerves of steel."

Adam Roberts agrees. He used to head the US chapter of the British-based Born Free Foundation, which operates a 75-hectare (186-acre) sanctuary for almost 550 primates near Dilley in south central Texas.

Running a sanctuary "is not for the uninitiated and the unprepared," says Roberts. "We get contacted at Born Free all the time by people who say, 'I want to start a sanctuary.' And we try to dissuade them unless they're really prepared. But most of them aren't. Some people are able to do it as they go, and it works. But those people are rare... The success rate for people

who have no previous experience is very, very low."

Usually the problem is money. When you factor in the cost of land, food, veterinary bills, upkeep, and staff, it can cost hundreds of thousands or even millions of dollars a year to run a sanctuary. And all of it comes from donations. Neither the government of Canada nor of the US pays a penny toward maintaining animal sanctuaries. It all comes from the big hearts of people who love animals and want to see them cared for. But what happens when such people fall on hard times and no longer have money to give? What's a sanctuary to do then?

This male iguana resides at the Wildlife Rescue & Rehabilitation sanctuary. Once victimized by the wild animal "pet" trade, he was one of the fortunate ones to be turned over to a sanctuary where he will live as a permanent resident. WILDLIFE RESCUE & REHABILITATION, INC.

HELP FOR THE HELPERS

Kellie Heckman runs the Global Federation of Animal Sanctuaries (GFAS) in Washington, DC. It's an international non-profit organization that helps sanctuary operators when they run into trouble. GFAS inspectors also inspect sanctuaries throughout the world to make sure they meet certain standards. They look at the quality of the animal care, how well the sanctuary is run, whether there is enough money to pay for everything, and if there's a plan in place if something goes wrong. After their review, GFAS will offer guidance, training, and advice, because they want to make sure that all sanctuaries can support the animals in their care for each animal's lifetime. Heckman estimates that no more than one in ten of all the so-called sanctuaries in the US and Canada meet GFAS standards.

Those are the ones run by the truly one-in-a-million miracle workers who not only established a sanctuary—the easy part—but have kept it going, too. These are the extraordinary individuals who have what it takes to provide homes for animals who would otherwise end up who knows where.

IN 1996, David Mallory, a lumber baron from Gore Springs, Mississippi, took possession of 38 lions, tigers, and cougars from a big-cat collector named Catherine Gordon Twiss. The cats were in terrible shape after a lifetime of abuse and neglect, but Mallory established a sanctuary for them called Cougar Haven.

The sanctuary was paid for by Mallory's business, but when the economic crash of 2008 hit, Cougar Haven was hit too. Suddenly the cash to run it was gone. Corners were cut and living conditions collapsed. Soon there was barely enough food to keep the cats alive.

By the end of 2009, only three—two tigers and a liger (a cross between a lion and tiger)—remained. Eventually, GFAS was called in to rescue Cookie and Alex, the fourteen- and fifteen-year-old tigers, and Freckles, the fifteen-year-old liger. All three were transported to Big Cat Rescue, a sanctuary near Tampa, Florida (more about it in Chapter Four), where they live to this day.

Mallory's former neighbours were pleased to see the cats go because they knew they would be looked after properly. One neighbour said he would miss the cats' morning roars, but his wife, who had spent days in the hospital after being bitten by one, would not.

THERE ARE exotic animal sanctuaries all over the world. Many other countries have places where animals rescued from the pet trade, the entertainment world, or the destruction of their habitat can go to be looked after. For the last twelve years, GFAS has handed out an annual award to the sanctuary that it believes best meets its vision of excellence in animal care, called the Carol Noon Award for Sanctuary Excellence. As of 2019, six of those awards went to countries outside North America. They were the UK, Uganda, Costa Rica, China, Vietnam, and Indonesia. All the rest were in the US.

WRR's cougar enclosures include rocky ascents and natural terrain that helps provide a more enriching life for the permanent resident cougars. WILDLIFE RESCUE & REHABILITATION, INC.

The Chimpanzee Sanctuary Northwest in central Washington state has indoor and outdoor enclosures. Here, Jamie goes for a walk outside. PHOTO COURTESY OF CHIMPANZEE SANCTUARY NORTHWEST

2

OUR CLOSEST COUSINS

A girl wants to look her best, which is why Thiele is checking herself out in this compact mirror at Chimps Inc. in Oregon. PHOTO COURTESY OF CHIMPS INC.

TOBY WAS A gentleman. Not every chimp is, but Toby was. He liked to wear a scarf. He enjoyed the company of female chimpanzees, and they enjoyed his. Rachel, a former laboratory chimp, was his constant companion. They liked to while away hours sitting side by side on a bench, grooming each other. He was even known to dabble in the arts. He once painted a mural that still enjoys pride of place in his last home, the Fauna Foundation, a 1.6-hectare (4-acre) sanctuary for eleven chimps, twenty minutes east of Montreal.

Toby died suddenly in October 2017 of what vets believe was heart failure. But before his death, the 40-year-old black chimpanzee was always content at Fauna. He had a collection of watches that he loved to put on so he could watch the second hand go around and around. He also loved musical instruments, especially ones he could bang. He banged the tambourine like Animal from *The Muppet Show*. He was partial to dark chocolate, potato chips, and muffins, which sanctuary staff baked for him, as well as the raspberries, strawberries, and blackberries that grow in Fauna's gardens. But he never had to pick them; staff did that for him, too.

But life for Toby wasn't always easy. He was born at a roadside zoo near Montreal that sold him to an unaccredited zoo in northern Quebec, where winter lasted half the year. The snow

Toby looks out a window at the Fauna Foundation near Montreal. Fauna is the only chimpanzee sanctuary in Canada.
FAUNA FOUNDATION

fell in drifts, and darkness arrived in the middle of the afternoon, which meant Toby had to stay in his cell for two-thirds of the day, every day. His only pleasure was his cellmate, Benji, whom Toby loved like a brother. Benji was born at the zoo, but his mother rejected him, so zoo staff placed him with Toby instead. They became great favourites with zoo visitors. In summer, they dressed in clothes and paraded around their enclosure like a couple of millionaires, smoking cigarettes and drinking soda. Zoo patrons had their pictures taken with them.

Then something strange happened. After about two years, Benji's mother wanted Benji back. In fact, she broke into the enclosure where Benji and Toby lived and moved in with them. Amazingly, the arrangement worked. All three chimps were happy. Benji had his real mother back, and Toby had a mother figure. They lived this way for almost 21 years and may have lived for 21 more if Benji's mother hadn't contracted pneumonia and died. Suddenly, Toby and Benji were on their own again, grieving the loss of someone they loved.

Then, two years later, disaster struck again. During one of the hottest summers Quebec had ever known, when the mercury was rising like a rocket, Benji died of thirst, passing away in Toby's arms.

Toby was devastated. He screamed and cried. He had been with Benji his whole life and couldn't face living on his own. So the Fauna Foundation, one of eleven chimpanzee sanctuaries in North America and the only one in Canada, rescued him. But he was still traumatized. He didn't eat. He didn't respond to attention. He just curled up in a ball and hid from everyone and everything. The staff decided to take a chance and introduce him to a pair of older females, Sue Ellen and Donna Rae, who they hoped would look after him. They did. As soon as Toby saw them, he ran into their arms. They saved him. He was invited into their world and followed them wherever they went.

Intellectually, chimps are as clever as three- or four-year-old children, but unlike children of that age, they're potentially dangerous. A 70-kilogram (150-pound) chimpanzee may be smaller than an adult man, but he's up to seven times stronger. And he may not think twice about attacking someone if the mood strikes. That's why

Toby relishes the thought of eating a banana as he sits among the greenery at the Fauna Foundation outside Montreal. FAUNA FOUNDATION

if you visit a chimpanzee sanctuary—a rare experience, since most are deliberately located in out-of-the-way places and barred to the public—the first thing you do is promise not to blame the sanctuary if anything goes wrong. It's also why you're told never to go near the chimps or attempt to touch them.

▲ Chimp Haven in Louisiana has the largest outdoor chimpanzee enclosure on the continent. The area is covered in pine trees that are native to the state. CHIMP HAVEN

➤ Chimps are excellent climbers and love to be up high. Here, Emma takes a look down at the grounds of Chimp Haven. CHIMP HAVEN

LEARNING ABOUT
PEOPLE THROUGH CHIMPS

The first zoo chimp to be imported into North America was a female named Polly, who was captured in Africa and brought to the Bronx Zoo in 1902. More chimps followed, but it wasn't until 20 years later that the first research chimps were introduced to America. They were brought to Florida in 1923 by a psychologist named Robert M. Yerkes, who spent his entire adult life (he died in 1956) studying chimps in captivity.

His work prompted researchers all over America to start using, and abusing, chimpanzees, too, in experiments that were meant to tell us more about ourselves than chimps. While people would have objected to performing such experiments on humans, they had no such qualms about using chimps. You see, chimps are our closest biological cousins. In fact, they are 98.4 percent genetically identical to us. It is now thought that it was only 6 million years ago that chimps and humans became two distinct species. It isn't surprising that, for years, scientists regarded them as the next best research subjects to humans themselves. They were used in drug trials, in experiments involving diseases, even in the space program. In the late 1950s, at a New Mexico Air Force base, a breeding colony of 65 chimps was used to test the effects on their brains of high speed, high-altitude travel, extreme pressures, and even space flight. Chimps were strapped into spinning capsules, tied down in decompression chambers, and ejected from aircraft while travelling at the speed of sound. In 1961, two chimps named Ham and Enos were shot into space. Both were injured and scared witless, but their mission was declared a success.

However, it wasn't until the 1980s that chimp research really exploded. At the time, many people were dying of a disease called AIDS, and scientists thought that because chimps are so similar to humans, they would be ideal research subjects. They weren't. Chimps don't exhibit any AIDS symptoms, so studying them was pointless. But as many as 2,000 chimpanzees had been imported into US laboratories for the express purpose of learning about AIDS. What was to become of them?

Killing them was out of the question. By then, public feeling had changed quite completely since the dark days of Dr. Yerkes. People no longer agreed with harming chimps, precisely for the same reason that Yerkes had for utilizing them: because they are so like us. An alternative

Sarah takes a quiet moment away from the hustle and bustle of Chimp Haven to enjoy the sight and smell of a couple of red roses. CHIMP HAVEN

research done on them had to be for the benefit of chimps, not people. That effectively put an end to all experiments on chimpanzees.

The problem is that about 600 chimps still live in laboratories across the US (there are none in Canada). The sanctuary system isn't big enough to accommodate them all. Captive chimpanzees live for about 50 years. That means many laboratory chimps will die before they get a chance to live anywhere else. Others will be luckier because sanctuary space is opening slowly. A number of sanctuaries in the US hope to have new places available for them soon.

had to be found. First, people stopped breeding chimpanzees in America, and no more thought was given to capturing them in Africa. Second, land for chimpanzee sanctuaries was found and bought in different parts of the country by people who wanted to help them. And third, the so-called CHIMP Act, which became US law in 2000, made it illegal to kill chimpanzees except for human health reasons. In 2015, the US government went a step further by declaring captive chimps "endangered," meaning that any and all

LIFE AT CHIMP HAVEN

Chimp Haven, a sanctuary near Keithville, Louisiana, boasts outdoor enclosures that, at 2.2 hectares (5.5 acres), are among the largest in North America. Elm and pine trees grow in them. In the morning, chimps climb these trees, groom each other, and rest. Then, after lunch, it's time for enrichment exercises. These can be food puzzles where the chimps find food hidden away in some object, or they could involve bubble machines, wind chimes, disco balls, lava lamps, crayons and chalk, or television. Chimps at Chimp Haven love TV.

Arthur sits atop a culvert in one of several large Save the Chimps enclosures in Florida. The enclosures are full of objects like this culvert that make life more interesting for the chimps. SAVE THE CHIMPS

They will huddle around it, like football fans on Super Bowl Sunday, to watch nature videos, cartoons, and anything in which people fight. Chimp culture can be aggressive and their fondness for fighting mirrors that. But even a chimp can be soothed by music. Musicians are invited regularly to play for them. Among the many performances at Chimp Haven were a drum circle, a violin concert, and a ukulele demonstration. Do the chimps listen? Caretakers say it depends on the animal. Some couldn't care less, while others hang on every note.

By 4:30 or 5:00 PM, it's bedtime. Chimps sleep longer than humans. Where they sleep—outdoors or in—depends on the animal, but chimps always make nests for themselves. Chimp Haven caregivers have identified more than 200 in the sanctuary's forest, most of which have been made using materials available on the ground and in the trees.

This structure was specially constructed by staff at Save the Chimps in Florida so that chimpanzees like Kiley and his family would have a place to climb and rest. SAVE THE CHIMPS

ISLAND CHIMPS

Only one chimp sanctuary is larger than Chimp Haven. In fact, it's the largest chimpanzee sanctuary in the world. Save the Chimps, on the east coast of Florida, is home to close to 250 chimpanzees. Like Chimp Haven's residents, they came from research and biomedical labs, the entertainment industry, the pet trade, and the US Air Force.

The chimps at Save the Chimps live on one of twelve islands, 1.2 to 1.6 hectares (3 to 4 acres) in size. Because of the way their muscles are configured, chimps can't swim. Put them in water and they sink like an anchor. On islands, they are in an environment from which they can't escape. But each island is connected by a bridge to a six-room chimp house. That way, chimps have access to both the indoors and the outdoors. Each island has native

Florida trees growing on it—palms and evergreens—as well as various man-made climbing structures and culverts for shade. The most populated islands have more than 20 chimps living on them.

Every week, chimps at Save the Chimps eat 873 kilograms (1,925 pounds) of apples, 1,020 kilograms (2,250 pounds) of bananas, 380 kilograms (840 pounds) of oranges, and 426 kilograms (980 pounds) of tomatoes.

THE PROBLEM WITH CAPTIVITY

Because zoo chimps, lab chimps, and pet chimps can never be returned to Africa, a sanctuary is the best place for them. But they still have to be locked up in enclosures, which, caregivers say, is uncomfortably close to locking up people.

Diana Goodrich, the co-director of Chimpanzee Sanctuary Northwest in Washington State, says one of her chimps, Jamie, "seems more aware of being captive than the other chimps. She also seems more demanding and will ask more from us than the other chimps will. As her caregiver, our relationship is definitely complicated. It's not straightforward at all. We're friends with [the chimps] and we interact with them. They ask us to interact with them. But we're also the ones

You never know why chimps will do the things they do. Burrito, the only male resident at the Chimpanzee Sanctuary Northwest in central Washington State, carries a brush in his mouth as he goes for a walk. CHIMPANZEE SANCTUARY NORTHWEST

in control of their lives, so they rightfully react to that."

It means, Goodrich says, that Jamie may even resent her. "I would say of any of [the chimps], Jamie might think about that. About us doing things to them that they have no control over."

JAMIE, A CHIMP who lives in a sanctuary in Washington State, has a thing for cowboy boots. Not a day goes by when the 40-year-old, charcoal-grey female doesn't demand that the people who look after her indulge her obsession.

The ritual starts with Jamie instructing her caregivers to put on a pair of cowboy boots of her choosing. Unfortunately, she doesn't care a thing about sizing, so if the boots don't fit, that's the wearer's problem, not hers. Then they'll go for a walk around the sanctuary's 0.8-hectare (2-acre) outdoor enclosure.

The walk takes ten to fifteen minutes through the tall grass and breezy air of summer, after which the boots come off. Then Jamie will grab a stick to clean them. She wants them to look pristine for the next walk, which might begin as soon as she's finished. If the weather's fine, it's not unusual for Jamie and her crew to walk around the enclosure twelve to fifteen times. And each time Jamie will be as delighted as she was the time before.

Jamie, who lives at the Chimpanzee Sanctuary Northwest in central Washington State, has a thing for boots. She loves them. In fact, every day she insists that the sanctuary's volunteers put their boots on and go for a walk with her. CHIMPANZEE SANCTUARY NORTHWEST

CHIMPS INC. in central Oregon is also a chimpanzee sanctuary, but instead of labs, its chimps were raised in houses as pets. In other words, they were raised by humans to be as human-like as possible.

They'd sit at the table with their adoptive humans. They'd go for rides in the family car. They'd eat the same food that the family ate. They'd play with toys and wear clothes intended for children. In short, they grew up as people, not chimps. Except they weren't people. Chimps are wild animals, and eventually that wild side comes to the fore. It isn't uncommon for chimps who once watched TV in the family living room to suddenly find themselves locked in cages not much bigger than they are. Topo, Chimps Inc.'s first resident, was kept in a windowless shed for 20 years before being rescued by founder Lesley Day in 1995.

But even though Chimps Inc.'s chimps are wild at heart, they're still a product of their upbringing. You can take the chimp out of the suburbs, but you can't take the suburbs out of the chimp. Consequently, the chimps at Chimps Inc. brush their teeth every day. They like to wear clothes, hats, and jewellery and to have their finger- and toenails painted. They eat with a fork or spoon. And they play videogames on an iPad.

▲ Most of the chimps now living at Chimps Inc. in Oregon used to be pets so they're used to wearing human accessories like sunglasses. CHIMPS INC.

▼ Jackson is at his coolest in this pair of wraparound sunglasses as he chills out in one of the outdoor enclosures at Chimps Inc. in Oregon. CHIMPS INC.

28-year-old Christopher is one of the first two orangutans at the Center for Great Apes in Florida, arriving when he was only five years old. CENTER FOR GREAT APES

3

MONKEY BUSINESS

Pierre, an olive baboon who lives at the Story Book Farm Primate Sanctuary in Ontario, is a guide to young monkeys entering the sanctuary for the first time. He'll show them around and help them when they have problems. DAINA LIEPA

FOR A FEW days before Christmas 2012, Darwin was the most famous monkey in the world. The young Japanese snow monkey, or macaque, was found wandering around an IKEA parking lot in Toronto wearing a boxy faux shearling coat and a badly soiled diaper. He had arrived at the parking lot with his "mom" in a crate in the back seat of her SUV, but when she left to go shopping, he broke out of the crate and opened the car door. Then he was free.

Shoppers couldn't believe their eyes. They started filming Darwin on their smartphones. Then they posted the videos to YouTube, which resulted in Darwin, or the "IKEA monkey," as he became known, going viral. The Internet practically groaned from all the views. He was on the news, too.

Everyone thought he was adorable. Everyone, that is, except Toronto Animal Services, who arrived at the scene wearing gowns and filter masks. They said Japanese macaques carry a type of disease that is dangerous to humans and didn't want to risk contracting it. When they captured him and took him away to the Story Book Farm Primate Sanctuary, an hour and a half northeast of the city, they were careful to stay as far away from him as possible.

Meanwhile, his "mother," Yasmin Nakhuda, was beside herself. She said young monkeys are completely dependent on their mothers and have to be with them 24 hours a day. That meant

LEFT Once upon a time, Darwin was the most famous monkey in the world when he was discovered in the parking lot of a Toronto IKEA. Now he lives the life a monkey should live at the Story Book Farm Primate Sanctuary. DAINA LIEPA

RIGHT Pockets, whose full name is Pockets Warhol, after the great American pop artist Andy Warhol, helps raise money for the Story Book Farm Primate Sanctuary by painting pictures that the sanctuary sells for $350 each. CHARMAINE QUINN

Nakhuda, a real estate lawyer, took Darwin to work with her. She took him shopping. Every night she bottle-fed him milk and changed his diaper. There is even video of them standing together brushing their teeth. She sued the sanctuary to win him back. Trouble was, keeping exotic animals like snow monkeys is illegal in Toronto (it's legal in other parts of Ontario but not Toronto) so the judge trying the case had little sympathy for Nakhuda. The following September, Justice Mary Vallee ruled that Darwin should remain in the sanctuary and that Nakhuda should no longer keep

exotic animals in the Toronto suburb where she lived.

Today, Darwin is an adolescent living under the guiding hand of an older baboon named Pierre. Just like any adolescent, Darwin needs to be shown the ropes now and then, and Pierre is there to oblige. A relationship like theirs is important to Darwin, since he never had the chance to learn anything from his real mother.

But also like any adolescent, Darwin likes to get out and have fun. He likes to throw balls, swing, climb, jump, and run. He's very active and strong—he can bend a thick steel wire using his claws—and his teeth are needle sharp. He also likes dogs. Strange people make him nervous, but dogs delight him. He loves it when volunteers bring their pooches to the sanctuary.

Darwin is one of seventeen monkeys who live on Story Book's two-hectare (five-acre) property. There are capuchins, squirrel monkeys, lemurs, rhesus macaques, Japanese macaques, and spider monkeys. At the centre of the property is a building that houses the monkeys' indoor enclosures. Radiating out from it are a number of outdoor enclosures that can get pretty cold in winter. But Darwin doesn't mind. After all, he's a snow monkey.

Inside is a playhouse full of diversions. There are climbing structures, fire hoses, tires, tree branches, heat lamps, mirrors, and stuffed animals to hug, groom, or tear to pieces. Pierre enjoys leafing through magazines.

And Pockets, a white-capped capuchin, likes to paint. One day, for no special reason, one of Story Book's volunteers decided to let Pockets try his paw at wielding a brush. She had no particular reason to think he would be any good at it, but he took to it like Picasso. In fact, the sanctuary now has a gallery where Pockets's paintings are displayed. He paints about one a week and sells about 20 a year. They cost $350 each.

Rudy is a squirrel monkey who lives at the Story Book Farm Primate Sanctuary. Ordinarily, squirrel monkeys live in the tropical jungles of Central and South America, but thanks to the pet trade, Rudy has ended up living in Canada. DAINA LIEPA

It gets hot in Texas, so monkeys living at the Born Free USA Primate Sanctuary, like this bonnet macaque, are always grateful for some water to drink or play in. BORN FREE USA, SHANAY DICKEY

MONKEY BARS

Story Book is one of several monkey sanctuaries in North America. The Born Free USA Primate Sanctuary mentioned in Chapter One is another. In fact, it's one of the best primate sanctuaries in the world, but there's no hiding the fact that it looks pretty scary from the outside. It's the fence. It's so big and formidable that it looks like something you'd have to be crazy to approach. But that's deliberate. There are almost 550 monkeys living at Born Free, and just like residents in a fortress, they are well protected. Former sanctuary director Tim Ajax helped see to that. After all, monkeys are nothing if not curious, so you have to be constantly on guard when you have hundreds to look after. In that way, Ajax was king of the Born Free castle.

But in every other respect, the sanctuary is a monkey wonderland. It is 75 hectares (186 acres) in size, and there are grasses and shrubs everywhere. Almost

These Japanese macaques are the direct descendants of a group of macaques who were flown to Texas in the 1960s. They now live at the Born Free USA Primate Sanctuary. BORN FREE USA, PAULA PEBSWORTH

everywhere else are mesquite trees. Mesquite trees don't grow very tall—like apple trees—but Born Free's monkeys love to climb them. They also produce beans that the monkeys eat. And because monkeys can never get enough of climbing, there are also plenty of man-made climbing structures that the monkeys like.

Three species of baboon live at the sanctuary along with seven species of macaque and three species of vervet (a medium-sized monkey from Africa known

to exhibit several negative human traits, including hypertension, anxiety, and if alcohol is made available to them, alcohol abuse). But the different species don't live together. They don't mix like monkeys in the jungle do. Instead, the sanctuary is divided into enclosures where monkeys live with other monkeys of their own kind. The largest of these enclosures (22 hectares, or 56 acres) is for the Japanese macaques, or as they're more commonly known, snow monkeys—like Darwin. It's

▲ Ernie is a long-tailed macaque living at the Born Free USA Primate Sanctuary. He's in no mood to share his pumpkin. BORN FREE USA, SHANAY DICKEY

➤ Herbie and Kirby are a pair of squirrel monkeys enjoying life at the Jungle Friends sanctuary in Florida. The sanctuary is full of plants and trees that make it seem almost like a jungle. JUNGLE FRIENDS

bigger than any other enclosure because there are more Japanese macaques in the sanctuary than any other type of monkey.

To understand why, you have to go back to Japan in the 1950s and 1960s, when Japanese primatologists set out to study macaques in their own environment. But because snow monkeys are shy, the scientists didn't have much luck. So they tempted them with food. As a result, not only were the monkeys less reclusive, they started having more babies. In fact, their population grew to a point where they split into two groups, one of which moved out

of the forest and into the city of Kyoto. Residents were furious. So much so that the Kyoto government threatened to kill the macaques.

And it would have, were it not for a monkey-loving Texan named Edward Dryden, who said they could live on his ranch instead. Getting there involved lots of twists and turns, but in 1972, the monkeys were deposited on Dryden's large Texas acreage, where they would be looked after until they died. Today's Japanese macaques are their descendants. Eventually, other kinds of monkeys were introduced to the Born Free USA Primate Sanctuary, but it was the macaques—and Dryden—who gave birth to it.

The other monkeys at the sanctuary have come from the pet trade, roadside zoos, and laboratories. There are more than 100,000 monkeys in North American laboratories and hardly any of them end their lives in sanctuaries. Most are killed. But sometimes people working in labs grow attached to them, so when the monkeys outlive their usefulness, their minders ask that they be sent to a sanctuary. And sometimes they are.

MONKEYS FOR SALE

It's hard to believe that anyone would be foolish enough to purchase a monkey as

a pet, but if you search "monkeys for sale" on the Internet, you'll find many sites where you can buy tamarins, capuchins, marmosets, squirrel monkeys, and more. But you'll pay a lot for them. Depending on the species, a young monkey can cost more than $5,000. Then there are the accessories: the primate stroller, the diapers, the baby bottles, and the cute little onesies that will make your little simian look like a human baby.

But no matter which website you visit, they all have one thing in common. They only sell babies. Why? Because you can control a baby monkey. You can't control an adult. By the time monkeys are five or six years old, they will do whatever they want—including bite your face. It's not surprising that owners of older monkeys often feel totally overwhelmed. Sometimes the situation gets so bad that the owners end up keeping their monkeys in a locked cage. However, a few are lucky enough to be given to a sanctuary like Story Book, Born Free, and in Florida, Jungle Friends.

▲ Mila is a capuchin living at the Jungle Friends sanctuary. You can see plainly that she's in a cage, but she still has plenty of room to climb and run and stretch her legs. JUNGLE FRIENDS

➤ Allie and Louie live in the only orangutan sanctuary in North America, the Center for Great Apes in Florida. One of the things orangutans like most is fresh fruit. CENTER FOR GREAT APES

JUNGLE FRIENDS

Jungle Friends is a 17-hectare (42-acre) primate sanctuary and rehab centre in the central part of Florida. More than 300 monkeys, representing twelve species, live on the property in more than 200 enclosures. The size of the enclosure depends on the size of the monkey, the monkey's needs, and the number of monkeys it houses. For example, the marmoset enclosure may seem small, but given how tiny marmosets are (at about 141 grams, or 5 ounces, they are the smallest monkeys in the sanctuary), it's actually quite big. Meanwhile, the spider monkey enclosure is gigantic by comparison, simply because spider monkeys are gigantic by comparison (they weigh about 9 kilograms, or 20 pounds).

There are also trees and plants everywhere. The monkeys have to live in enclosures to be safe, but because the enclosures are in a forest, they don't look or feel like cages. Leaves and branches poke through them like fingers through a tennis racquet. When you visit Jungle Friends, you see oaks, bamboo, banana plants, and other trees in every direction. They envelop the sanctuary like a cloak. They also attract birds and bugs, which enrich the monkeys' lives and help create a more natural environment. Jungle Friends employees also do their part by outfitting the enclosures with sand pits, mulch, perches, trapezes, rope ladders, and hammocks.

About half the monkeys at Jungle Friends come from laboratories. The rest began life in zoos, circuses, or as pets. For example, Jersey Boy is a former pet capuchin who arrived at age nine with a missing toe and a left leg so badly damaged it had to be amputated. Now he uses his tail as a kind of second leg and gets around fine. Udi, a spider monkey, was rescued from a dingy New York apartment when he was a year old. He was later diagnosed with a disease that gave him soft bones. Consequently, his wrists turned out and his spindly legs were bowed. But doctors said that with exercise, sunlight, and a special diet, he would be fine. And he is.

This is the mission of Jungle Friends— to look after its monkeys to the highest physical, psychological, and emotional standards that it can. Yes, emotional. That may sound strange, but if you've ever interacted with a dog or cat, you'll know it isn't. You know when the dog or cat is happy, sad, worried, angry, or frightened. It's the same with monkeys. Research into animal emotions confirms this. Sanctuary owners know they have to make their animals mentally and emotionally healthy, as well as physically well. After all, that's what makes life worth living.

THE CENTER FOR GREAT APES

The same is true of the Center for Great Apes, the only accredited sanctuary in North America for orangutans. Located 90 minutes south of Orlando, Florida, the centre is a 50.5-hectare (125-acre) paradise of dense wilderness (oaks, maples, mango trees, and more) and orange groves. Chimpanzees live on the property too, making it the only sanctuary in North America where orangutans and chimpanzees live together. (There are no North American sanctuaries for gorillas or bonobos.)

The sanctuary has twelve large jungle-gym-like structures for the animals to climb on and hang from. Some of these enclosures—or habitats, as they're called—are huge. Just like at Jungle Friends, they all include an assortment of climbing structures, swinging vines, toys, tubs, culverts, and other objects to enrich the apes' lives. There is even an enclosure devoted exclusively to apes who are disabled or old.

Each habitat also has what's called a night house. These provide the animals with a place to sleep at night and rest during the day. They all have high nesting areas, hammocks, and beds. They also function as safe places for the apes—retreats from the hot Florida sun or even from hurricanes when they barrel in from the Atlantic.

Finally, all twelve habitats and night houses are connected to each other by a system of elevated tunnels or skywalks that meander through the property for more than 2.4 kilometres (1.5 miles). These tunnels in the air give the apes the sensation of running through the jungle as they move from one habitat to another. They also like seeing what other apes and staff are up to.

The Center for Great Apes was founded by Patti Ragan in 1993 when she was asked to temporarily care for a four-week-old male orangutan named Pongo at a Florida tourist attraction. She expected him to go to a zoo when his owners came back for him, but when he got sick, they told her she could keep him. But she had no idea what to do with him. After all, there was no such thing as an orangutan sanctuary then, so she did the only thing she could. She started one of her own.

Today, Pongo is a strapping lad of over 122 kilograms (270 pounds). The only home he's ever known is the Center for Great Apes, so he has no idea what it would be like to live in the wild. But he has the next best thing: He's safe, well fed, entertained, and loved.

THERE ARE MORE than 260 different kinds of monkeys in the world, and they are as varied in size and shape as humans. The world's smallest monkey is the pygmy marmoset, which weighs only 113 grams (4 ounces) and stands at only 12 centimetres (5 inches) tall. The world's biggest monkey is the mandrill, which weighs 35 kilograms (77 pounds) and is 1 metre (3 feet) tall.

Monkeys eat both plants and small animals, including birds' eggs, insects, spiders, and even tiny lizards. They live in trees and groups. Monkeys in a group will protect each other, help each other find food, and care for each other's young. A group of monkeys is known as a mission, a tribe, a troop, or a cartload.

IN MALAY, the language spoken in Malaysia, "orang" means "person," and "utan," derived from the word "hutan," means "forest." So "orangutan" means "person of the forest."

Orangutans have tremendous arm strength, which enables them to hang from tree branches for long periods of time. This is important because they spend most of their lives in trees. Their arms can also be very long. The arms of large males can stretch 2.5 metres (8 feet) from fingertip to fingertip. Like humans, orangutans have opposable thumbs that enable them to grip branches and other objects. But unlike humans, they also have opposable toes, so they can cling onto things with their feet.

Pebbles is an orangutan enjoying some of what's on offer at the Center for Great Apes in Florida. There are all sorts of things to climb on, which is what orangutans love. CENTER FOR GREAT APES

Carole Baskin is the founder and CEO of Big Cat Rescue in Florida. Here, she's pictured having a chat with one of the many tigers in her care. BIG CAT RESCUE

4

FUR, FANGS, AND CLAWS

In-Sync Exotics near Dallas is a sanctuary for all kinds of big cats, including leopards like Jett. IN-SYNC EXOTICS

NORMAN BUWALDA was a big man who loved big cats—African lions and Siberian tigers. In fact, Buwalda, who lived in the small southwest Ontario community of Southwold, kept a collection of lions and tigers as pets. No one ever knew exactly how many he had, but there were always several living in large chain-link cages behind his house.

Buwalda kept the cages locked because he knew his cats were dangerous, but that didn't stop him from walking them around his property—much to the dismay of his neighbours. They didn't like living next door to cats as big as Harley-Davidsons, and they especially didn't like it when those cats were taken out to be exercised.

In 2003, a group of neighbours petitioned the township to make keeping big cats illegal. It was for the safety of the community, they said. Someone could get hurt or even killed. But the council disagreed. So what if Buwalda walked a tiger around his property, they said. He wasn't bothering anyone, and no one had ever been hurt.

Until someone was.

A year after the neighbours made their plea, a ten-year-old boy was invited onto Buwalda's property to take pictures of his cats. Buwalda released one of his tigers from its cage so the boy

Leopards love to perch in trees. They like to be up high so they can see what's going on below them. Simba, who died a number of years ago, is pictured here catching a snooze in one of the trees growing at Big Cat Rescue in Florida. BIG CAT RESCUE

could get a better look at him, and the tiger attacked. Buwalda swore the cat was under control, but the boy was badly injured.

Suddenly, the council couldn't act fast enough. Within a month, it passed a comprehensive ban on the keeping of large and deadly cats (alligators too), and said the tiger who attacked the boy had to be put down. You might think that would have been the end of Buwalda's zoo, but you'd be wrong. What the council hadn't counted on was Buwalda's decision to challenge the ban in court, which he won in 2006. The provincial court judge trying the case ruled that the ban violated Buwalda's right to do what he wanted on his own property.

Even then, the story wasn't over. Four years later, the same tiger who had wounded the boy mauled Buwalda to death. Buwalda had entered the tiger's cage to feed him, and the tiger pounced. No one witnessed the assault, so no one knows why the cat did what he did. But the outcome was indisputable. One of the tigers whom Buwalda had fought so hard to keep ended up killing him.

For a while the case received massive publicity. People were amazed that the Province of Ontario allowed people to keep tigers as pets. It still does. It depends on the municipality or city or town, but there is still no province-wide law that says tigers and other dangerous animals cannot be kept on people's private properties.

What happened to Buwalda's cats remains a mystery. One day they were there, and the next they weren't. The only thing that can be said with certainty is that they didn't go to a large-cat sanctuary in Canada, because there aren't any. There are a few roadside zoos that keep large cats in cages scarcely bigger than the cats themselves, but there are no accredited sanctuaries that provide big cats with the kind of care they need. Those are all in the United States.

Most good sanctuaries have some kind of medical facility on their property. Here at Big Cat Rescue in Florida, this tiger undergoes a complicated procedure to keep him healthy. BIG CAT RESCUE

BIG-CAT SANCTUARIES IN THE US

The quality of big-cat sanctuaries varies from city to city and state to state. No

Sometimes animals have to be moved around within a sanctuary. Here, a cougar is put on the back of a truck at Big Cat Rescue in Florida. BIG CAT RESCUE

one can say with any certainty how many institutions there are in the US that say they give lifetime care to lions, tigers, and leopards, but there may be about 200. The trouble is that most of them are really just unaccredited zoos. In fact, according to GFAS there are only nine large-cat shelters that offer large cats real sanctuary.

One of them is the Wild Animal Sanctuary, 56 kilometres (35 miles) northeast of Denver, which is home to 70 lions, 55 tigers,

5 leopards, and 2 jaguars, all of whom live on ground that once belonged to the buffalo. It also houses 180 bears as well as several foxes, coyotes, ostriches, emus, and horses, and a camel. At 291 hectares (720 acres), it is the largest and oldest large carnivore sanctuary in North America. And while it may sound as if it cares for a lot of cats—132 in total—compared to the number of large cats living in zoos, circuses, and private households, it's only

a drop in the ocean. No one really knows how many captive large cats there are in North America, but educated guesses put the number around 10,000. And most of them—maybe 8,000—are tigers. Why? First, people who keep large cats seem to like to show off, so why not show off the biggest, baddest cat of all? Second, tigers are easy to breed so there is a constant supply of them. And third, tigers are worth a lot of money when they're killed to make traditional Asian medicine.

Big Cat Rescue in Tampa, Florida, has 76 cats in its care: 24 bobcats, 3 caracals (long-eared medium-sized cats native to Africa, the Middle East, and Asia), 7 cougars, 5 leopards, 3 lions, 2 Canadian lynx, 15 tigers, 2 hybrid cats (these are created when one species of cat breeds with another, such as a lion with a tiger), 1 Siberian lynx, 11 servals (leopard-like cats native to Africa), and 1 genet (a small, spotted, long-tailed cat, also native to Africa). They eat 226 kilograms (500 pounds) of meat a day.

When Carole Baskin, the founder and CEO of Big Cat Rescue, established the sanctuary more than 25 years ago, it was in the middle of nowhere. There were trees and fields on every side of it. Now, as a sign of the times, the 27-hectare (67-acre)

You may not know it, but tigers love water. That's why Cincinnati, a tiger living at the In-Synch sanctuary in Texas, has his own pond to play in. IN-SYNC EXOTICS

facility is surrounded by malls, subdivisions, and freeways. When you enter Big Cat, you enter through the gift shop, called the Big Cat Trading Post, where you can buy all things big-cat-related, gift cards and glassware, T-shirts, and toys. You can also visit the cats at Big Cat Rescue (income from tours help pay the $3.5 million it costs to keep the sanctuary going every year), but you have to go with a guide. Because enclosures may go back hundreds of feet, there's no guarantee you'll see

Lambert was bought by a family in Texas because the family's children, who had just seen *The Lion King,* wanted their own Simba. It wasn't long before he was rescued by In-Sync Exotics near Dallas. He still lives there today.
IN-SYNC EXOTICS

anything. Remember, this is a sanctuary, not a zoo, so if the cats don't feel like showing themselves, they won't.

Actually, each cat lives in two enclosures connected by a door. The biggest is a full hectare (2.5 acres) in size, but most are 1,200 square feet (111 square metres, about the size of a large two-bedroom apartment). The overall landscape is woodland, so it's shady. Good thing, since Florida gets awfully hot in summer. Most cats live on their own, but there are exceptions. Five serval cats share an enclosure, as do two leopard sisters, Armani and Jade. (Armani is so beautiful that she has appeared in both *Glamour* and *People* magazines.) There is also a lion and white tiger pair, Cameron and Zabu, who grew up together in a roadside zoo and couldn't be parted when they arrived at Big Cat.

IN-SYNC EXOTICS

In-Sync Exotics has 75 cats and 2 lemurs living on 5 hectares (13 acres) near the town of Wylie, a suburb of Dallas, Texas. There are 35 tigers, 6 lions, 11 cougars, 4 leopards, 1 cheetah, 2 lynx, 12 bobcats, 3 servals, and 1 ocelot. They came from zoos, circuses, and the pet trade. One lion named Lambert was bought for two kids who had seen *The Lion King* and wanted their own Simba.

Now the cats are being looked after in a way that only a good sanctuary can. In-Sync is mainly grassland, but there are also pecan trees everywhere, providing much-needed shade in summer. Depending on the size of the cat, enclosures range from 370 to 1,500 square metres (4,000 to 17,000 square feet), the equivalent of two good-sized suburban lots. Whether a cat lives by itself also depends on the cat. Some like company; some don't.

Bakari, who lives at the Lions Tigers & Bears sanctuary in California, came to the sanctuary when he was only four weeks old. He got his name from a pair of sanctuary supporters who knew that Bakari is an African name that means "one with great promise." LIONS TIGERS & BEARS

The enclosures are also outfitted with toys to make the cats' lives more interesting. For example, all tiger enclosures have pools because tigers love water. And

▲ Conga the leopard lives at the Lions Tigers & Bears sanctuary. She began life as a captive-bred pet who was abandoned by her owners when she was only five weeks old. That's when she was adopted by LTB. LIONS TIGERS & BEARS

➤ It may not be Africa, but at least the cats living at Lions Tigers & Bears near San Diego, including this lion, have natural places in which to roam and be themselves. LIONS TIGERS & BEARS

all cougar and leopard enclosures have above-ground platforms because cougars and leopards like to be up high. Motorcycle tires hung from trees make great swings for all cats, but for some reason lions are especially fond of them. They also have huge exercise balls, which they chase, destroy, and then have replaced. The tigers also have big blue discs to lie on in their pools, and all the cats have boxes

because, as anyone who's ever lived with a cat knows, cats love boxes. In summer, when the temperature can reach almost 40 degrees Celsius (100 degrees Fahrenheit), they get ice cubes. At Christmas, they get trees decorated with paper towel tubes, streamers, and leaves.

LIONS, TIGERS, AND BEARS, OH MY!

Lions Tigers & Bears is located 1,200 metres (4,000 feet) up the slope of the Cuyamaca Mountains in San Diego County, California. 65 animals live on the 38-hectare (94-acre) property, including four tigers, three cougars, six African lions, three leopards, a serval, three bobcats, and an Indian jungle cat (a medium-sized, russet-coloured cat that hunts small mammals and birds). There are also ten bears.

Founder and director Bobbi Brink opened the sanctuary in 2003 after seeing an advertisement in Texas selling lions, tigers, and bears. She answered the ad and found the animals crawling around the floor in a mobile home. "They were just being used and abused," she said. So she decided to do something about it. She started volunteering in sanctuaries until she was ready to open one of her own. When she was, she chose the California town of Alpine because it's her home and because "these animals need someone to be their voice and they need a place to go when things go wrong."

Like In-Sync, Lions Tigers & Bears tries to keep its residents stimulated by adding variety to the enclosures they live in. In fact, it isn't unusual for animals to switch enclosures every three or four days so they can enjoy different views, different smells, and different surfaces. The overall landscape is meadow-like, with lots of grass, oak trees, and large rocks placed here and there, like a rock garden. Each enclosure is unique. Some have pools. Some have trees. Some have grass. Some have toys. All have logs. The point is that each one is different.

NO VISITORS ALLOWED

Seven of the nine large-cat sanctuaries accredited by GFAS allow visitors; two don't. They are WildCat Ridge in northwest Oregon and the Wildcat Sanctuary in eastern Minnesota. It's not that their operators think people observing their cats would harm them; it's that they've decided their cats will never be exhibited again.

Take Nikita, a female white tiger. As a cub, Nikita was removed from her mother and put on the end of a chain so people could have photos taken with her. Her owner was a notorious tiger breeder who had been in prison for cocaine and steroid trafficking and illegal gun

A caracal is a medium-sized wild cat native to Africa, the Middle East, and Central Asia. This one, named Aurora, enjoys the birch, beech, and pine forests of the Wildcat Sanctuary in eastern Minnesota. WILDCAT SANCTUARY

possession. When Nikita was too big to photograph any more, he confined her to a small, concrete-floored cage with another tiger. He beat both of them regularly. Eventually, however, he died, and Nikita was rescued.

"When it comes to cats like Nikita, who have had an incredibly traumatic life, we know they recover faster and learn to trust again when they are able to live in a quiet and calm environment," says Jeanna Hensler, the outreach coordinator for the Wildcat Sanctuary. "For cats like her, being at a sanctuary that is open for tours would have severely impeded her recovery."

VISITORS WELCOME

By contrast, the Wild Animal Sanctuary near Denver gets as many as 150,000 visitors a year. Sanctuary officials have decided that it doesn't upset its 450 animals to be looked at. Visitors follow an overhead walkway and look down on the sanctuary's residents, who seem to barely notice them. There are 67 enclosures. The biggest, which contains a pride of lions, is 10 hectares (24 acres) in size. The smallest is five.

Every year the sanctuary rescues 40 to 70 new animals. It can do that because it's so large. But even then, there's a limit to how many animals it can keep. Too many animals would mean crowded enclosures, and that would turn Wild Animal into something more like a zoo than a sanctuary.

A sanctuary habitat may sound massive compared to a zoo enclosure, but sanctuary owners know that compared to the African savannah, a sanctuary is a mere garden. Carole Baskin of Big Cat Rescue explains it this way: "One of our enclosures is an acre (about four city lots). Two are half an acre. The biggest one is two and a half acres. It sounds big, doesn't it? Until you stop and realize that, in the wild, a tiger would have 400 square miles (1,000 square kilometres or an area a little smaller than the city of Los Angeles)."

ONE OF the most popular legends in all cat lore is that of the royal white tiger, the one-of-a-kind cat with white fur instead of orange. It is said that in the wild only one in every 10,000 tigers is white, which is why they are so highly prized.

But should they be? Usually white tigers are the result of in-breeding—father to daughter, mother to son, sister to brother. This can cause crossed eyes, clubfeet, kidney problems, arched or crooked backbones, and twisted necks. White tigers are also said to be less fertile than orange tigers and more likely to miscarry. Even in the wild, the white tiger's life is more dangerous because he or she lacks the camouflage that orange fur provides.

In fact, because of this, the US Association of Zoos and Aquariums barred member zoos from breeding them in 2011. Former Wildlife Conservation Society director William G. Conway said: "White tigers are freaks. It's not the role of a zoo to show two-headed calves and white tigers."

IN 2011, the Wild Animal Sanctuary experienced the largest rescue of big cats in its history when 25 circus lions dropped out of the sky.

In 2010, the government of Bolivia made it illegal to use animals in circuses. The Wild Animal Sanctuary agreed to give the country's 25 circus lions a new home.

On February 16, a transport plane carrying 25 cages touched down at Denver Airport, each one containing a lucky, if slightly bewildered, former Bolivian circus lion.

Today, the 32 hectares (80 acres) set aside for them are divided into four 8-hectare (20-acre) habitats, where the lions live in prides. All the habitats have prairie grasses as well as trees. Structures have also been built for the lions to climb and lie on. But their primary enrichment comes from each other and the other animals in the sanctuary.

You could be forgiven for thinking that you're looking at a black panther. However, Shadow, who lives at the Wildcat Sanctuary in Minnesota, is actually a rare black African leopard. WILDCAT SANCTUARY

The reticulated python is the largest snake in the world. They can grow to be more than 6 metres (20 feet) long. And yet they are still available as pets in North America. This one, named Willy, lives at the Forgotten Friend reptile sanctuary in Pennsylvania. FORGOTTEN FRIEND

5

SCALY SURVIVORS

Jesse Rothacker is the founder and director of the Forgotten Friend Reptile Sanctuary in Pennsylvania. The young alligator he's holiding, named Chet, will very quickly grow a whole lot bigger than he is now.
PHOTO COURTESY OF FORGOTTEN FRIEND

YOU'D NEVER KNOW there was anything unusual about Val Lofvendahl's house if you drove by it in 2019. It looked like most of the other houses on a fairly busy street in suburban Vancouver, BC. Biggish, whitish, and newish, with lots of room for a car. But if you opened the door, the light would be soft and dim, and the room you'd walk into would be warm, but with barely any furniture in it. Instead, it had rows of glass terrariums, all about the size and shape of a microwave oven, and all with some kind of reptile inside. Most were snakes (corn snakes and ball pythons), but there were lizards too (bearded dragons and leopard geckos).

Lofvendahl ran a facility called the Reptile Rescue Adoption and Education Society until she retired in 2019. All of her reptiles were rescued, and Lofvendahl had a website and Facebook page where she advertised the animals, hoping to find new homes for them. She also took them to reptile shows where prospective adopters might have been looking for exactly what she had. It was a slow process, but with luck and time, she was able to find new guardians for the reptiles she'd been taking care of for months before.

People are always getting rid of reptiles, Lofvendahl says, because they don't want to care for them. At first, they think it would be cool to have a snake or lizard draped over their shoulders. Then cool becomes a chore. Pet shops know this. That's

Bugatti, named after the classic French sports car, is one of five tortoises enjoying the good life at the Cleveland Amory Black Beauty Ranch in Texas. The sanctuary, America's largest, is also home to tigers, horses, pigs, bears, cougars, camels, chimps, hippos, and many other animals. BLACK BEAUTY RANCH/THE FUND FOR ANIMALS

why they sell monitor lizards when they're small enough to fit into your palm. What they don't tell you is that it doesn't take long for that pinkie-sized infant to grow into a five-foot colossus.

NO SUCH THING AS A GOOD REPTILE SANCTUARY?

Clifford Warwick, a British biologist who specializes in reptile biology, welfare, and protection, says there could be as many as 13 million pet reptiles living in the US, with hundreds of thousands more in Canada. And it's hard to think of even one, he says, who doesn't lead a miserable life. That's because most of them live in cages or terrariums. Even with the best possible care, the animals will still suffer, he says, because they live in terrariums not much bigger than themselves.

Even so, many people still think it's okay to treat reptiles this way, Warwick says, because they're cold and scaly instead of warm and fuzzy. It's easy to think a terrarium is an appropriate home for them. But once when we get to know them, we realize it's not.

Science has shown us that reptiles are a good deal more complex than anyone realized. For example, experiments done in Britain and the US show that reptiles have much better memories than anyone expected. They also can solve rudimentary puzzles and learn by imitation, something scientists thought only more advanced animals could do.

These are some of the reasons why Zoocheck, a Toronto-based animal protection organization, says there's no such thing as a good reptile sanctuary. Zoocheck believes that by keeping reptiles in small terrariums, as most sanctuaries do, they're depriving them of the ability to be their natural, complex selves.

Nelle enjoys one of two iguana rooms at the Cleveland Amory Black Beauty Ranch in Texas. The neighbouring room has a swimming pool as well as a number of hammocks for the iguanas to rest in. BLACK BEAUTY RANCH/THE FUND FOR ANIMALS

EXCEPTIONS TO THE RULE

There are, however, a couple of exceptions to this rule. The first is the Cleveland Amory Black Beauty Ranch in Murchison, east Texas, which has five tortoises (four African spurred tortoises and one leopard tortoise) and four green iguanas (three females and a male), all rescued from the pet trade. And they are all living the best kind of life captivity has to offer. The sanctuary is America's largest and is also home to tigers, bears, cougars, camels, chimps, hippos, horses, pigs, and many other animals.

The tortoises live in a large, warm house—which Black Beauty staff call the Tortoise Taj Mahal—and have a tenth of a hectare (quarter of an acre) on which to roam. The sanctuary is located in the piney woods of Texas, so there are several pine trees and lots of green grass in the enclosure. There are also plenty of shrubs and burrows that the tortoises dig up. Turkeys, ducks, and chickens parade through the enclosure as well, so every once in a while, you might just catch the bizarre sight of a tortoise chasing a duck.

The indoor enclosure includes two rooms. One has a heated pool, and the

This eastern box turtle lives at American Tortoise Rescue in California. That means he's a long way from home. In the wild, eastern box turtles live, as their name suggests, in the eastern US, but as pets they can end up anywhere. AMERICAN TORTOISE RESCUE

perch on. Staff try to place plants from the iguanas' native South and Central America in the room, but the lizards eat them so quickly that they never have a chance to grow. The second room has a swimming pool, some hammocks, and more perches. There's also an outdoor area for when the temperature rises above 18 degrees Celsius (65 degrees Fahrenheit), which it often does in Texas.

The second US reptile haven is located thousands of kilometres west of Black Beauty in one of the most exclusive enclaves in the country. Susan Tellem and her husband, Marshall Thompson, run the American Tortoise Rescue in Malibu, California, the celebrity capital of the world. So many Hollywood stars pass by their door—Lady Gaga, Britney Spears, and Liam Hemsworth among them—that they don't even notice them anymore. To them, celebrities have become as commonplace as grass. Besides, they have other things to look at. The American Tortoise Rescue area teems with native plants, flowers, bees, butterflies, hummingbirds, doves, and parrots, and two roosters rescued from Malibu Beach. They also have about 100 tortoises and turtles, who give the property its name.

other is a sunroom that allows in a special kind of light that helps the tortoises absorb the nutrients in their food more efficiently. Tortoises don't swim, so the pool is only fifteen centimetres (six inches) deep. They use it to soak themselves and ease their digestion.

The iguana house also has two rooms. The main room is three metres (ten feet) high with skylights in the ceiling and a series of platforms for the iguanas to

Like the Reptile Rescue Adoption and Education Society did, the American Tortoise Rescue used to place tortoises and turtles in new homes. In fact, in 27 years it has rescued and rehomed more than 4,000. But now the organization is strictly a sanctuary. None of the animals living there are physically fit to be rehomed (some have difficulty eating, while others are missing a foot or even feet), so they live with Tellem and Thompson instead. And Tellem and Thompson do everything they can to make their lives comfortable. In addition to enjoying such luxurious surroundings, the tortoises and turtles have houses to sleep in. The large tortoises, who grow to be a half a metre (a foot and a half) long and 36 kilograms (80 pounds), have their own houses. Smaller turtles share. There can be as many as 25 small turtles in one house. There is also a turtle hospital.

The animals eat every other day. The turtles eat worms, insects, fruit, and vegetables. The tortoises eat greens, bananas, strawberries, and other fruit. They all enjoy basking in the sun until it gets too hot, at which point they go into a house for a midday siesta. Otherwise they roam the property continually, quarrel sometimes, and even mate. Any eggs laid are eaten by gophers. And all of them are different, says Tellem. "They're individuals," she says. "They're not rocks with legs. People don't realize that they all have personalities."

The Black Beauty Ranch and the American Tortoise Rescue are special in

This American alligator is currently living at the Forgotten Friend reptile sanctuary in Pennsylvania. But he won't be there forever. Once alligators grow to a certain size, they're transferred to sanctuaries in Georgia or Florida, where there's more room for them. FORGOTTEN FRIEND

the reptile world in that they're in a position to give homeless reptiles the kind of lives that homeless chimpanzees and tigers enjoy. Most reptile sanctuaries are not like this. They are usually small, crowded, overwhelmed facilities where reptiles, and occasionally amphibians, are warehoused in small cages and terrariums. There are dozens of such sanctuaries in Canada and the US.

THE LIMITS OF
REPTILE SANCTUARIES

The Forgotten Friend Reptile Sanctuary near Lancaster, Pennsylvania, is in farming country, where fields are thick with corn or soybeans. In fact, Forgotten Friend is rather like a small farm itself, with a house and two garages. One garage is for owner Jesse Rothacker's children to play in, and the other is for his 100 or so reptiles and the occasional amphibian. Rothacker will sometimes get frogs, toads, and salamanders, but because they're so delicate, they represent only about two percent of the animals he takes in. Most other reptile sanctuaries are the same.

Forgotten Friend sits on about 0.4 hectares (1 acre) of land, meaning iguanas, monitor lizards, and native turtles can sometimes stretch their legs outdoors. However, this is only true in summer. Remember, reptiles are cold-blooded, so they can't survive snow—and it snows a lot in Lancaster. Only native box and painted turtles will bury themselves under it to hibernate. Rothacker also keeps alligators, but only until they're 1.5 metres (5 feet) long, after which they go to sanctuaries in Georgia or Florida that can better accommodate them.

Half of Rothacker's reptiles are snakes (none of them venomous) and the rest are turtles, tortoises, lizards, and alligators. They all live in stackable plastic cages with sliding plastic doors, but Rothacker believes they're happy that way. "Taking a snake that was born in captivity, and housing him in an appropriate cage, with appropriate heating and lighting and enrichments, can be a fulfilling life for that animal," he says.

Several dozen species are represented at Forgotten Friend. There are geckos, bearded dragons, iguanas, boas, pythons, king snakes, corn snakes, rat snakes, milk snakes, and hognose snakes. There's even a 4-metre (13-foot) reticulated python, the largest snake in the world. It weighs 45.4 kilograms (100 pounds) now, but if it keeps growing it could be a gargantuan 9.75-metres (32-feet) long and 160 kilograms (350 pounds) one day.

Rothacker routinely takes his animals to school assemblies, church halls, medical conferences, and birthday parties to show them off (for money) and to demonstrate to people what's involved in keeping reptiles. Because, astonishingly—and despite the fact that all his animals began life in the pet trade—Rothacker believes it's okay to keep reptiles as pets.

"I have supported legislation to prohibit the sale and purchase of alligators as pets, because I don't believe the majority of them can be kept safely and humanely in captivity. But I don't support banning most reptiles as pets, though, because most of them can be kept safely and humanely as pets," he says.

Rothacker got his first reptile—a snake—when he was a boy, and he hasn't looked back since. He's also been bitten more times than he can count. He decided to open Forgotten Friend in 2004 after learning how to run a sanctuary from veterinarians, zoo officials, cat rescue groups, and others. There was no rescue centre for reptiles and amphibians in Lancaster then, so Rothacker knew one was needed. He was right. In no time, he and his wife weren't able to handle the volume of calls they got. They still can't.

CREEPY CRITTERS

Across the country in California, about an hour and a half south of San Jose, is Creepy Critters, an 8-hectare (20-acre) sanctuary in the middle of some of the hottest, driest country you'll find in the United States. It can be a sizzling 46 degrees Celsius (115 degrees Fahrenheit) in summer and, for many of the 600 or so reptiles and amphibians who live at Creepy Critters, that's

It won't surprise you to learn that Chinese water dragons are native to China. This one lives at Creepy Critters Rescue in California, though, and it's hardly the size of a dragon. The biggest Chinese water dragons only to grow to be about one metre long. CREEPY CRITTERS RESCUE

too hot. It's why some of them are kept indoors where the climate is controlled.

Ask Creepy Critters founder Jennifer Ramsey about pet stores and reptiles, and she'll tell you a lot. Pet stores, she says, have no clue how to look after a reptile or amphibian. They're usually staffed by people who may get an afternoon's training in pet care, if that. In other words, they're in no position to offer reptile advice to anyone. Is it any wonder, she says, that so many buyers dump their animals onto people like her?

Tortoises like this one at the Creepy Critters sanctuary near San Jose, California, can live a long, long time. Some species can live over a hundred years. That's another reason why you should never adopt one as a pet. Who's going to look after it when you're dead? CREEPY CRITTERS RESCUE

But it isn't just pet owners who ditch their animals; stores do it too. Any reptiles they can't sell they present to Ramsey to look after. But they do it without giving her a penny for their upkeep. The local SPCA does the same.

"People get interested in [reptiles]," Ramsey says, "and then, like anything you collect, they get carried away. They want rare animals and complicated animals to show off. But they don't know how to look after them. So, they end up coming to people like me."

That's why for Zoocheck founder Rob Laidlaw, the issue is clear. There is no

way, he says, that reptiles and amphibians should ever be kept as pets.

"The reptile and exotic animal pet trade is a largely wasteful and unnecessary industry," he says. "Species are being driven to extinction, ecosystems are being disrupted, and millions of individual animals are being forced to suffer."

And yet, the trade continues. Millions of snakes, lizards, turtles, and tortoises are bred each year in Canada and the US for sale. And they end up in places like Val Lofvendahl's rec room, safe and cared for, but living in terrariums scarcely bigger than they are.

GENERALLY SPEAKING, tortoises are bigger than turtles and have bigger shells. A tortoise's shell is also more dome-like than a turtle's, which is more streamlined. Tortoises have small sturdy feet and bent legs. Turtles have webbed feet and long claws designed for swimming.

Tortoises live on land and never go near water, except to bathe and drink. Turtles spend all or most of their lives in water.

Tortoises are vegetarian, while turtles eat small fish, insects, and worms.

Mother turtles lay their eggs on land and then head straight for water, leaving their eggs unprotected. Mother tortoises guard their hatchlings for up to 80 days.

Tortoises also live longer than turtles. While most turtles live 20 to 40 years, tortoises live for more than 80. Some live to be 150.

THE PINE ISLAND Audubon Sanctuary in North Carolina is different from all the other sanctuaries mentioned in this chapter because it's a sanctuary for native wildlife, including reptiles and amphibians. 1,052 hectares (2,600 acres) of wilderness—forests, fields, and marshes—have been set aside to preserve such reptiles as cottonmouth moccasins, black racers, ribbon snakes, rainbow snakes, snapping turtles, box turtles, and mud turtles, and such amphibians as green frogs, bullfrogs, American toads, and green treefrogs.

It is also a haven for bobcats, otters, mink, coyotes, foxes, and all kinds of birds.

Tortoises, like this one living at the Creepy Critters sanctuary near San Jose, California, are vegetarians. They love vegetables like squash. Turtles, on the other hand, eat insects and small fish in addition to vegetables. CREEPY CRITTERS

The Performing Animal Welfare Society elephant sanctuary in California is a beautiful place full of shade-giving trees, tall grass and big skies. PAWS

6

A PROBLEM THE SIZE OF AN ELEPHANT

Mara, one of eight elephants living at the
Performing Animal Welfare Society in
California, is almost exactly the same colour
as the tall grass she's walking through. PAWS

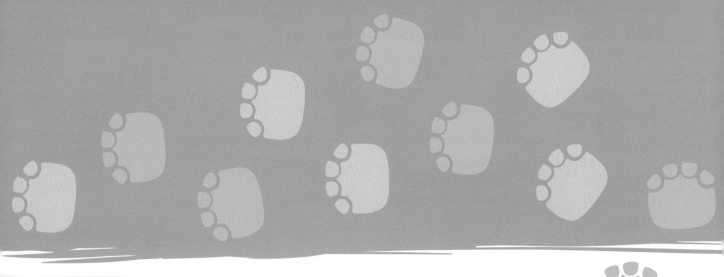

THERE WAS MUCH trumpeting on the day Thika, Toka, and Iringa arrived at the Performing Animal Welfare Society (PAWS) elephant sanctuary in California. The three resident elephants—Maggie, Lulu, and Mara, all of whom had lived at the sanctuary for years—stopped what they were doing to watch. PAWS is a beautiful place where the elephants live rich, comfortable lives, but when you've been in one place for years, a surprise is always welcome. So when Thika, Toka, and Iringa appeared out of nowhere on that brilliantly sunny October day in 2013, Maggie, Lulu, and Mara were there to greet them.

Thika, Toka, and Iringa had just spent the last four days and nights travelling on two trailer trucks from the Toronto Zoo in Ontario to the almost 49-hectare (120-acre) PAWS elephant sanctuary near Sacramento. The sanctuary was a different world. Their zoo enclosure was barely 0.8 hectares (2 acres) in size; the sanctuary was 60 times as big. The zoo was flat, concrete, and empty of greenery; the sanctuary was hilly and covered in grass and trees.

Not only that, because of age and arthritis two of the three zoo elephants hadn't lain down in years. If they had, they wouldn't have been able to get up. But at PAWS, they could lean against a soft 45-degree hill and take half their weight off their

▲ Toka is one of three lucky elephants who were removed from the Toronto Zoo and sent to the Performing Animal Welfare Society in California. PAWS

➤ Debbie and Ronnie are two of the eleven elephants currently living at The Elephant Sanctuary in Tennessee. They have 2,700 acres in which to roam, far more than any zoo could provide. THE ELEPHANT SANCTUARY IN TENNESSEE

feet. Also, there would be no one staring at them. They could just be themselves, elephants being elephants.

But it took two years to get them there.

It all began in 2011, when the board of the Toronto Zoo, the premier zoo in Canada and one of the best-known zoos in North America, decided to close its elephant exhibit. Seven elephants had died in the zoo's elephant enclosure—one had killed another—and the three who remained—Thika, Toka, and Iringa—were in poor health.

Zoocheck asked the zoo to send the elephants to PAWS. It was by far the best option, they said, because it would provide the best life for the elephants. Zoocheck even flew PAWS's founder, Ed Stewart, to Toronto so he could speak to the zoo board. The board declined to hear him, but Toronto's city council was so impressed that it voted overwhelmingly to send Thika, Toka, and Iringa to PAWS. And the sooner, the better.

But the zoo objected, citing a number of concerns. One was that they felt the journey to California was too long, especially if it was made by truck—the elephants wouldn't have sufficient opportunity to rest, exercise, or lie down. It was a legitimate worry. After all, elephants were never meant to travel in trucks. They were meant to live in jungles and grasslands in Africa or Asia. But now that they're in North America, the way they usually get around is by truck, although a few travel by train as well. In fact, because of those concerns, zoo staff recommended sending the elephants to another zoo in Florida, a trip that would take only half as long. On the surface it sounded like a reasonable option, until you consider the proposed destination: a zoo, not a sanctuary.

The zoo also said PAWS wasn't accredited by the US Association of Zoos and Aquariums, which was true. However, sanctuaries don't fall within the remit of the AZA, so even if PAWS wanted its accreditation—which it didn't—it couldn't get it.

Zoocheck believes that at the root of the zoo's objections was the tension that often exists between zoos and sanctuaries. This tension is a byproduct of the fact that zoos, despite the often valuable conservation work they do, are primarily businesses (they charge visitors admission and make every effort to make sure that animals are visible to those visitors), while sanctuaries exist solely for the welfare of their animals. (A few sanctuaries do permit visitors to see their animals, but most don't. If you recall, PAWS allows them only four times a year.) Consequently, sanctuaries can be critical of zoos, and this criticism can foster bad feelings.

As it turned out, the Toronto Zoo managed to put off sending the elephants to PAWS for a whole year. But when that year was up and the matter came up for a second vote, even more councillors elected to send Thika, Toka, and Iringa to PAWS. This time, the zoo had no choice but to comply.

The journey to California was 4,100 kilometres (2,500 miles) long. Travelling with the elephants was a trainer, a manager, two veterinarians, and the head of Zoocheck. Because the elephants weren't in the best of health, transporting them such a long distance was a risky undertaking. No wonder the Zoocheck campaigns director, Julie Woodyer, cried when they arrived safe and healthy.

Sadly, Iringa had to be put down two years later. She had painful joint problems from living on hard surfaces in Toronto's snowy climate for so many years, and she never recovered. But Thika and Toka remain at PAWS to this day, two of eight elephants who call PAWS home.

PAWS is one of two elephant sanctuaries in North America that are accredited by GFAS. The other is the Elephant Sanctuary in Hohenwald, Tennessee. At the time this book was written, a third sanctuary, the newly opened Elephant Refuge North America, near Attapulgus, Georgia, was still awaiting its first elephant. An elephant named Mundi from the island of Puerto Rico was set to fill that role, but the island's government changed its mind at the last minute and held Mundi back. The refuge was established in 2019 by Carol Buckley, the same woman who co-founded the Elephant Sanctuary over 20 years ago.

With the eight elephants at PAWS and the eleven at the Elephant Sanctuary, there are currently nineteen elephants living in North American sanctuaries. That compares to the 430 or so living in zoos and circuses. It's also possible that a few are kept as pets.

TOUGH TIMES

Zoos vary in quality—some are dreadful, while others try to provide their animals with the best care they can—but none comes close to giving elephants the kind of life they'd lead in the wild. Wild elephants live in herds. In zoos, they often live alone. Wild elephants also like soft ground beneath their feet. In zoos, they frequently stand on concrete. And in the wild, elephants can travel up to 80 kilometres (50 miles) in a single day. In a zoo or safari park, the farthest they can go is a kilometre or two.

The lives elephants lead in circuses are even worse. In fact, it's probably the worst life an elephant can live. To begin with, circus trainers use violence and physical punishment to teach elephants tricks. They are also chained continuously. And when they do travel from show to show, they do so in cages not much bigger than they are, where they stand in their own feces and urine for hours at a time. As a matter of fact, things are so bad for circus animals that in 2019 the UK made it illegal for British circuses to use them anymore.

Part of The Elephant Sanctuary's landscape is a dense deciduous forest that the elephants like to explore. Here, Minnie and Ronnie stand at the edge of it. Ronnie has just pulled a big mouthful of grass out of the ground. THE ELEPHANT SANCTUARY IN TENNESSEE

But for a captive elephant, life in a sanctuary is the next best thing to life in the wild. In sanctuaries, elephants can lead lives that at least mimic the lives they would lead in Africa or Asia. They're always on soft ground, they move freely, and they have company if they want it.

LIFE AT PAWS

Walk through the main gate at PAWS and you'll see golden, grassy hills, oak trees, and pools of water reflecting a bright blue California sky. But because the place is so big, what you won't see are animals. With his trained eyes, Ed Stewart, PAWS's founder, sees them everywhere, but a casual visitor would swear there were none. What you can see are fences, tall sturdy ones built to withstand a bull elephant's heft and to separate one enclosure from another. The elephants have more than 48.5 hectares (120 acres) at their disposal, but those are separated into five enclosures, because not all the elephants living at PAWS get along.

The Elephant Sanctuary in Tennessee is so big that the eleven elephants who live there can choose to have company or not. Here, Tange enjoys some alone time as the sun begins to set on the sanctuary. THE ELEPHANT SANCTUARY IN TENNESSEE

Thika and Toka never liked each other, even when they were in Toronto. So now Toka lives with Maggie and Lulu in a separate enclosure from the one occupied by Thika and Mara. All five are African elephants. PAWS's three Asian elephants—two males and a female—also live in separate enclosures because Nicholas (a bull) might attack Prince (a neutered male) if they lived together. Meanwhile, Gypsy, the female, was exposed to tuberculosis when she worked in the circus and might still be contagious, so she has to be kept alone, too. Unfortunately, there's no way to know if she's still infected because there isn't an X-ray machine in the world big enough to scan an elephant.

At PAWS, the elephants spend their days grazing, tearing branches off trees, swimming, and covering themselves in clay. The African elephants particularly enjoy smothering themselves in the white clay

that bleeds through the soil. At night and when it gets cold, they often retire to a barn inside their enclosure. Hay, vegetables, fruit, and bran are always available, as is a sense of security. Because even an elephant needs to feel safe.

THE ELEPHANT SANCTUARY

The Elephant Sanctuary in Hohenwald, Tennessee, is built on 1,092 hectares (2,700 acres) of lush rolling hills, with tall grass, dense deciduous forest, and spring-fed lakes. The sanctuary provides individual elephants with medical care, the companionship of other elephants, and perhaps most important, the opportunity to live out their lives in as natural a setting as can be found in North America. And just as at PAWS, they can enjoy a bit of man-made comfort by retreating to the sanctuary's heated barns now and then. It gets awfully cold in Tennessee in winter and the elephants love a blast of artificially forced heat.

The Elephant Sanctuary also teaches people—both Hohenwald residents and visitors—about the plight of wild and captive elephants. On Hohenwald's main street is an educational centre called the Elephant Discovery Center.

"We do a lot of community outreach," says sanctuary spokeswoman Kate Mason.

"That's part of the reason for the existence of the Discovery Center. We do a lot of work with the local schools. Pretty much every class from Grades 1 to 12 has had some kind of interaction with the sanctuary. Children seem to understand the concept of a sanctuary better than adults. Adults are used to seeing elephants in captivity, but when you explain to a child why it's essential to let an elephant be free, they [get it]."

The irony is that no one is allowed to actually see the elephants. The sanctuary is not a zoo, so the only way you can view them is via one of thirteen solar-powered "EleCams" positioned throughout the grounds.

At the time of writing, there were eleven elephants at the Elephant Sanctuary. Over the years, it has been a safe haven for 28 animals. But unlike at PAWS, all its residents have been female. There are many more captive female elephants in North America than there are males because females are easier to train and handle than males. Also, the fencing at the sanctuary might not withstand the force of a male elephant, although the sanctuary is looking to change that.

The decision to retire an elephant to the Elephant Sanctuary or PAWS is never the sanctuary's to make. Only an elephant's owner may make that call, which is why Elephant Refuge North America couldn't do anything about the government of Puerto Rico changing its mind about Mundi. Sanctuaries will let owners know they have room for their elephants, but they don't have the right to seize them, even if they're being mistreated. That's up to the US Department of Agriculture or, in Canada, the SPCA, the Humane Society, the local animal services, or the police.

The Elephant Sanctuary is divided into three habitats, one for African elephants, one for Asian elephants, and, like PAWS, one for elephants exposed to tuberculosis. There are five such elephants at Hohenwald.

The 44 employees at the Elephant Sanctuary pride themselves on knowing that every day is different for their elephants. The reason is the sanctuary's size. It's so big that the elephants can choose to explore all or only a portion of it each day. It's also full of wild native animals, whom the elephants interact with as well.

A THIRD SANCTUARY

Carol Buckley and Scott Blais launched the Elephant Sanctuary in 1995, but Buckley left it in 2010. Now, as mentioned earlier, she has opened a new sanctuary, Elephant Refuge North America, in Georgia. It is 344 hectares (850 acres) in size and as private as Windsor Castle. Like the Elephant Sanctuary, it's made up of gently rolling hills, pastures, meadows, and dense forests. There are deer on the property, as well as bears, bobcats, raccoons, possums, bald eagles, great blue herons, and even an alligator. And soon, there will be elephants. Ten of them, Buckley hopes, both African and Asian. Buckley says that because elephants are at the top of every food chain, they will have nothing to fear from the wild animals living in the refuge since none of them would dare bother them.

Everyone who works with elephants says there are no other animals like them. Buckley describes them as highly evolved and incredibly wise. "Their energy is radiant, and they have a capacity for love that transports. When I'm in the presence of elephants, it's unexplainable. We don't know what the magnet is that draws us to them, but that magnet is definitely there."

But perhaps it was Pat Derby, Ed Stewart's late wife, who described the human—elephant bond best when she said, "I was born in love with elephants. Not for a reason that I know. Not because of any of their individual qualities—wisdom, kindness, power, grace, patience, loyalty—but for what they are altogether. For their entire elephantness."

LUCY, WHO LIVES at the Valley Zoo in Edmonton, Alberta, might be the most controversial elephant in North America. She is also its northernmost elephant. Edmonton winters are brutal, and Asian elephants were never meant to endure them. But Lucy does. She also lives alone, which is unheard of in the wild. Female elephants always live in herds.

Animal activists say Lucy is miserable, so they want the City of Edmonton to move her to one of the sanctuaries described in this chapter, but city and zoo officials refuse. They say she's happy and that moving her to a strange place—especially at the age of 49—would be disorienting and potentially dangerous.

So there she stands—day after day, year after year—the subject of intense debate and never-ending disagreement between animal activists, who want her moved, and city and zoo officials, who want to keep her where she is.

AFRICAN ELEPHANTS are much bigger than Asian elephants—up to 1,000 kilograms (2,200 pounds) larger. They also have larger ears. It's sometimes said the shape of an African elephant's ear is like a map of Africa, while an Asian elephant's ear is like a map of India.

African elephants also have tusks, while Asian elephants have small tusk-like teeth called tushes. An African elephant's trunk has two finger-like protuberances at its end that can be used to pick up and manipulate objects. An Asian elephant has only one protuberance. African elephants mainly eat leaves, while Asian elephants eat grass.

When Carol Buckley ran The Elephant Sanctuary, she would get very close to the elephants, including Tarra, who is pictured here giving Carol her trunk. Now Carol is about to open a new 344-hectare (850-acre) elephant sanctuary in Georgia, where she will keep ten elephants, both African and Asian. CAROL BUCKLEY

Sadly, parrots in captivity will often pluck the feathers out of their own bodies. They are so frustrated at being cooped up that they don't know what else to do. This cockatoo at the Oasis Sanctuary in Arizona is almost bald, but he still enjoys a good toy. OASIS

7

FOR THE BIRDS

Barney used to live at the Greyhaven Exotic Bird Sanctuary in British Columbia. He's since found a home, but when he was at the sanctuary he could whistle the theme to *The Addams Family* and imitate a telephone ringing. GREYHAVEN

BARNEY, A MOLUCCAN cockatoo who used to live at the Greyhaven Exotic Bird Sanctuary in Vancouver, is the reason owning a parrot may seem like such an attractive idea. Barney can whistle the theme to *The Addams Family* TV series. He can imitate a telephone ringing. He can shred a two-by-four piece of wood in the time it takes to say "Polly want a cracker," and then use the leftover chips to either scratch his head or unscrew the screws in his cage door. He's also affectionate. He loves to have his head stroked. When he wants your attention, he'll cock his head and coo, "Hello, Barney."

But there is another side to Barney. A side that may make you think twice about adopting a two-foot-long child of the wild with 227 kilograms (500 pounds) of pressure in his beak. He's moody. He may decide to bite you—hard—for no reason. He's also jealous. He hates it when you pay attention to other birds. He also might decide to pluck his feathers and yell with a force that may make you wonder if an Airbus has just taxied into your living room. Parrots are nothing if not vocal.

Much to the delight of Greyhaven staff and volunteers, Barney was adopted in 2019, despite these irritating habits. He was lucky. People who sell parrots rarely mention this side of living with them. If you search "Funny parrots" on YouTube, for example, you'll find lots of videos of parrots behaving in adorably. One

meows like a cat. One barks like a dog. One clucks like a chicken. No matter what they do, they're cute, charming, and irresistible, and you'll come away wanting one of your own.

It's the reason so many parrots are bred in captivity. As many as 2 million appear in the North American pet market each year, with prices as high as $1,500 per bird. There could be as many as 40 million living in North American homes at any one time—no one knows—and almost all of them began life as something to be bought, sold, or traded.

The awful irony is that while the number of captive parrots is exploding, the number of wild parrots is declining. As many as 130 of the world's 350 parrot species are endangered in the jungles of Africa, South America, Central America, Australia, and Asia. Strictly speaking, it's no longer legal to import parrots into North America or Europe, but because enforcement is so lax, they're still brought in by the thousands because so many people want chicks. Usually these chicks are placed into "parrot mills," where, once they get older, they will lay and fertilize eggs that will hatch into young birds that will be put up for sale. The birds range in size, from ones not much bigger than your finger to others as long as your arm, and in colour, from pink to white to green to purple to red to orange to blue.

In other words, while the birds may be beautiful, the business is not. Barney was rescued from a so-called sanctuary on Vancouver Island, where the owner kept up to 1,200 unwanted birds. Far too many to be looked after properly. Some lived in their own filth in small cat carriers. Others had their toes bitten off by other birds. Hundreds died from injuries and disease. It was supposed to be a happily-ever-after home for birds rescued from the pet trade, but it got too big too fast and it overwhelmed its owner. When she died in 2016, she left behind 584 birds of various sizes, shapes, and colours, who suddenly and desperately needed a home.

Enter Greyhaven. Normally Greyhaven cares for anywhere from 30 to 80 birds

▲ These budgies at the Midwest Avian Adoption and Rescue Services in Minnesota are chowing down on some muffins made specially for them. MAARS

◄ Sometimes parrots form a special, almost intimate bond with particular people. That's what's happened here between this cockatoo and this volunteer at the Greyhaven Exotic Bird Sanctuary in British Columbia. GREYHAVEN

in shelters located in two houses in Vancouver. But with the closure of the Vancouver Island refuge, Greyhaven was suddenly faced with the unprecedented challenge of rescuing almost 600 birds at once, making it the single biggest recovery of animals in Canadian history.

Fortunately, the story received a lot of media attention, so Greyhaven was able to start adopting out birds almost immediately. But it's hard to find a good home for a parrot. Not everyone is up for it. It takes patience, time, understanding, and love. Being young helps, too. Some species can live up to 100 years. That's why it isn't

unusual for a captive parrot to have as many as eight homes in his or her lifetime.

OFFICE BLOCK BIRDS

The Midwest Avian Adoption and Rescue Services (MAARS) sanctuary near downtown St. Paul, Minnesota, is home to 84 formerly abused, neglected, or abandoned birds. Located in—of all places—a three-storey former office building, MAARS houses birds as small as lovebirds (about the length of your hand) to macaws (about the length of a cocker spaniel).

This cockatoo lives at the Midwest Avian Adoption and Rescue Services (MAARS) sanctuary in downtown St. Paul, Minnesota. Not every parrot sanctuary allows its residents to go outside, but MAARS does. MAARS

The sanctuary moved into the building in 2009 after a year's renovation. Now each species has its own flight room, meaning there's an Amazon room, a macaw room, a cockatoo room, and so on. It's important to keep species separate because a large bird like a cockatoo could kill a small bird like a cockatiel. But the calculations don't end there. Just because you have two caged cockatoos living side by side doesn't mean you can let them loose in the same flight room. First, you have to make sure they'll get along. It's only then that you can house them safely.

But once that's sorted, the birds are allowed free run (or flight) of the place.

Walk along MAARS's main hallway, and there are birds everywhere. They're underfoot and overhead, talking and singing and calling to each other. Of course, that might be what you'd expect to see in a parrot sanctuary, but it's still an extraordinary sight—so many birds in such a small space in a downtown office block. Was there ever a jungle like it?

Each bird has a name and a distinct personality. Volunteers know these personalities well, which is essential because looking after the birds means more than just cleaning up after them. It means talking to them, petting them, playing with them, and making them feel loved.

Because that, more than anything, is what parrots want.

They also play with toys. For most of them, a toy is something to destroy. A block of wood. A series of boxes. A stack of paper plates. A piece of wicker. Parrots use their powerful beaks to slowly and systematically shred whatever is placed in their cages. It's good exercise for them and keeps their brains engaged too.

Some birds also have to be taught how to be birds. That may sound strange, but most captive parrots have only ever lived among people. So that's how they think of themselves—as people. Consequently, when they come to a place like MAARS, they have to learn to interact with other birds. To stay in the same flight room as another bird. To fly with another bird. It all takes time for a bird who's only spent time with people.

FOSTER PARROTS

The New England Exotic Wildlife Sanctuary, or as it's more commonly known, Foster Parrots, is another large parrot sanctuary. Located about half an hour from Providence, Rhode Island, Foster Parrots occupies what was once a 9.3-hectare (23-acre) chicken farm. It's home to as many as 400 birds, representing more than 50 species. There are also nine tortoises, an iguana named Zilla, and several turtles.

Unlike MAARS, the surroundings are rural. It's hard to see the sanctuary building at first because of all the trees. Then when you do, it's difficult to appreciate how big it is. But it is big—121 metres (400 feet) long and 12.1 metres (40 feet) wide. 90 percent of it is devoted to aviaries (there are 34, half of which have outdoor space), and 10 percent to the medical room, education hall, kitchen, and offices.

Some aviaries house just a pair of birds, while others accommodate entire flocks. Smaller birds, like parakeets, lovebirds, and cockatiels, flock naturally. But bigger birds—cockatoos and macaws—don't. In fact, they can be very territorial and may not tolerate company. If they do, it has to be a bird they like.

Every effort is made to make the birds' lives as interesting as possible with toys, flight areas, and one-on-one interaction. But as Foster Parrots staff readily admit, it's not and never will be the jungle. "Parrots are supposed to be out in the wild avoiding predators, socializing with other birds, finding food, and flying miles a day," says executive director Karen Windsor. It's why the people who run parrot sanctuaries say parrots should never be pets. They may be bred domestically, but their wildness stays in them.

Macaws are among the largest and most beautiful of all parrots. But they're also very territorial, so if they share a cage with another bird, it has to be a bird they like. FOSTER PARROTS

AN OASIS

The Oasis Sanctuary near the San Pedro River in the southwest corner of Arizona is an even busier sanctuary. It houses 794 parrots, representing 66 species, as well as 3 blackbirds, 2 pigeons, and a few chickens and waterfowl in 22 aviaries covering five hectares (twelve acres). The residents are from all over the US, but no more birds are being added to the sanctuary's wait list because it's already five years long.

Most of the aviaries have an open-air component and range in size from 4.6 to 371 square metres (50 to 4,000 square feet), which is big enough for 47 macaws. What makes Oasis unique is that most of its birds have medical problems that make them unadoptable. They may have wing injuries that prevent them from flying, they may be arthritic, or they may have deformed or stunted legs. Some problems are due to accidents or trauma, but some are due to captive breeding. The breeders mess with the birds' genetics, which leads to physical weaknesses.

But some problems are behavioural. Just as at MAARS, some of Oasis's birds don't know how to be birds because they were removed from their parents when they were too young. Breeders were once allowed to sell parrots when they were four to six weeks old. Now, the birds have to be four to six months old, but even that's too early when it comes to larger species. In the wild, African greys stay with their parents for a year. So do macaws. They need to because a young bird has so much to learn. "Years ago, domestically bred birds never learned to fly," says Oasis executive director Janet Trumbule. "That was the start of their inability to be social. They're taken from their parents at a young age and they don't learn how to be a bird."

Oasis birds eat fresh fruit and vegetables, nuts, popcorn, pumpkin seeds, and other healthy treats. And many of the parrots will use English words or phrases to speak to their caregivers. (A now-adopted parrot at Greyhaven spoke nothing but Spanish.) They'll ask for crackers or water. They'll also say their names and sometimes the names of the people or the dogs or cats they used to live with. One says, "Good morning, Doris" (presumably the bird's previous owner), and one, an African grey named Shadow, says, "You're a poop."

"YOU WON'T GET A PARROT FROM US"

Valerie and Ray Parkes care for about 60 parrots at Parrot Island Sanctuary in Peachland, British Columbia. Whenever Ray enters the 30-by-5-metre (100-by-16-foot) aviary he built specially for his birds, they screech with pleasure. No wonder. He dances with them. He takes them out for walks. He sings with them. He makes every one of them feel as special as he can.

Each is an individual, he says. "Some are quiet. Some are noisy. Some are aggressive. Some are lovey-dovey. Just like people."

When people visit the sanctuary, Parkes tells them, "If you're a young couple, you won't get a parrot from us. If you have young children, you won't get a parrot from us. Because [a parrot] doesn't make a good family companion. Usually, if it likes the wife, it doesn't like the husband. If it likes the husband, it doesn't like the wife. Or the kids. And that's the biggest reason people have to give up their birds. People say, 'I'm going to keep this bird forever.' They never do."

All of this matters to the Parkeses because, like Greyhaven, Parrot Island tries to rehome their birds. Over the years, the Parkeses have placed hundreds with "lonely mature people" who promise to devote themselves to the parrot.

Because parrots are so clever, they're not happy unless they have something to do. That's why this parrot cage at the Oasis Sanctuary in Arizona is so full of toys. OASIS

"I had one lady bring her dad here," Ray says. "She phoned me up and said, 'My mom passed away two years ago and my dad's so lonely. Please match him up.' So I matched him up with a bird. He had to come back several times to make sure the match was right. When he picked up the bird in a cage, I said 'Leave him in the cage for two weeks so that he can get to know his surroundings and get to know you.' That was on a Sunday. On Tuesday, I got an email with a photo attached of the bird sitting on his shoulder. He said, 'I've found my friend for life.'"

Even so, Parkes, like other sanctuary owners, doesn't believe in keeping parrots as pets. "To see them in the wild is the only way to see these birds. Is it really any life to live your life in a cage? I think we should stick to dogs and cats. An exotic bird should be left in its own country, flying wild and free."

PARROTS REQUIRE a lot of attention. They need to be talked to and played with regularly. They want to feel special. It's the reason Wesley Savoy of Parrots Forever, a parrot refuge in Edmonton, Alberta, has only sixteen birds. With just Savoy and his wife, Margo, to look after the parrots, they aren't in a position to have more.

From 4:00 PM, the time Savoy gets home from work, to 9:00 PM, the time the birds go to bed, he and Margo give each parrot one-on-one attention. They talk to them, stroke them, scratch them, carry them, and walk with them. "They just want to feel that I'm there for them," Savoy says. "They need all the one-on-one time I can give."

Budgies are very popular pets, but even they need to be rescued sometimes. It all depends on their owners. This yellow one lives at the Oasis Sanctuary in Arizona. OASIS

IT'S DIFFICULT to say how smart parrots are because parrots, like people, are individuals. They're all different. But one of the smartest parrots who ever lived was an African grey named Alex, who lived in Chicago with an animal psychologist named Irene Pepperberg.

Alex had a vocabulary of over 100 words, and he appeared to understand what all those words meant. He also could identify 50 different objects and recognize quantities of up to six items. He could distinguish seven colours and five shapes, and he understood the concepts of "bigger," "smaller," "same," and "different." Before he died, he was learning the difference between "over" and "under."

Who knows how much more Alex might have learned had he not passed away suddenly at the age of 31? Usually African greys live to be 60. The veterinarian who examined Alex's body couldn't find a cause of death, but it was later thought to have been a massive and sudden heart attack or stroke.

Alex's last words to Pepperberg were, "You be good. See you tomorrow. I love you."

At marine parks like SeaWorld, orcas are made to take part in shows that almost resemble circuses. PHOTO COURTESY OF JO-ANNE MCARTHUR/ WE ANIMALS

8

SWIMMING POOL PRISONS

Orcas are now a common sight in aquariums all over North America. Most are captive bred, but originally they had to be taken from the sea. This orca, however, remains where it belongs—in the ocean. RAINCOAST CONSERVATION FOUNDATION

THE SAD STORY of keeping orcas (also known as killer whales) in captivity began in November 1961 with a tragedy. A northeastern Pacific orca, subsequently named Wanda, was caught in the ocean and taken to Los Angeles by a team representing an aquarium called Marineland of the Pacific. Even though Wanda was 5.2 metres (17 feet) long, she was placed in an aquarium tank more suitable for walleyes (a fish about a metre long) than whales. It was the only tank available. But the moment she was placed in the water, she went berserk. She swam madly from one side of the tank to the other, bashing her head on the tank's walls. She did herself terrible harm, both internally and externally, but she wouldn't stop. She kept on swimming headlong into the concrete sides of the pool. Eventually, she did herself such damage that she died—less than a day after being captured.

Not surprisingly, it was another three years before anyone dared to capture an orca again. This time, the victim was a male named Moby Doll (his captors gave him a girl's name because they didn't know he was a male until he died). He was harpooned off the south coast of British Columbia. The hunters were looking for an orca to kill so a sculptor could use the body as a model for a statue for the new Vancouver Aquarium. But instead of killing

▲ More and more people are starting to object to keeping whales and dolphins in captivity, and they're letting their feelings be known at demonstrations, like this one outside the Vancouver Aquarium. JO-ANNE MCARTHUR/WE ANIMALS

➤ Belugas have joined orcas, or killer whales, as the whales of choice in marine entertainment centres and aquariums throughout the world. They have to spend their whole lives in a tank the size of someone's backyard. JO-ANNE MCARTHUR/WE ANIMALS

Moby Doll, they only wounded him. They could have struck him again and killed him, but for some reason they didn't. Instead, they towed him to a dry dock in Vancouver harbour, where for a short time, he was put on display. It was the first time an orca was put on public view. Officials had no idea how people would react to him, but he was a hit. On a single day in July, more than 20,000 people queued up to see him.

DANGEROUS CREATURES

Until the captures of Wanda and especially Moby Doll, orcas were thought to be dangerous creatures that people were taught to fear and harm. Their other name—killer whale—only added to their mystique. But that began to change, particularly with the capture of Moby Doll managed to survive a few miserable months in his Vancouver dry dock, despite

his wounds. Both scientists and the public began to look at Moby Doll with new eyes. Maybe, they began to say, it was wrong to kill orcas so thoughtlessly. (For years, fishermen shot at them because them claimed they were eating too much salmon.) Maybe, instead of doing what they could to rid the BC coast of orcas, they should be working to protect them.

Moby Doll's life in captivity was mercifully short, but the change he brought to the way we view and think about orcas has outlived him many times over. It is largely thanks to him that, instead of wanting to kill orcas, we now prefer to study and admire them. That's a good thing, of course, but back in the 1960s, 1970s, and early 1980s, when orcas became objects of fascination instead of horror, it resulted in some unexpectedly dire consequences. Suddenly, aquariums of all kinds wanted one, two, or even more orcas to show off to their patrons. It didn't matter how far away the aquarium was from the orca's habitat, it still had to have one. But how and where to get one?

WRESTLED FROM THE SEA

There was only one place and one way. They had to be captured from the wild. Teams of hunters went out in boats with nets and tanks, and literally wrestled them from the sea. No one gave any thought to how this would affect orca populations or orca families, or even the orcas themselves. They were just ripped from their worlds—their homes—for the entertainment of people from Vancouver to San Diego and Chicago to Orlando. SeaWorld, the most famous marine entertainment centre of all, was born on the backs of orcas. At its peak, dozens of orcas were housed in swimming pools the size of circus rings, in San Diego, San Antonio, and Orlando, where SeaWorld mounted its wildly popular marine shows.

The same thing happened to belugas (white whales native to the Arctic and sub-Arctic oceans), only it happened much earlier. In fact, it's thought that the first captive beluga was wrenched from the sea in 1860 for display at P.T. Barnum's American Museum in Manhattan. She lived only a few months, but again, as with orcas, a precedent had been set. Between 1860 and 1965, an estimated 30 belugas were captured from the Saint Lawrence River in eastern Canada for display in aquariums all over the United States. In 1979, Canada banned the capture of belugas from the Saint Lawrence, but by then, nets had long been cast elsewhere.

Twelve years earlier, hunters had transferred their operations north to the Hudson Bay, Canada's most famous body of open sea. Between then and 1992, the year Canada finally closed the hunt, hunters captured another 68 belugas for exhibit in aquariums in both the US *and* Canada.

Actually, the first two belugas to be displayed in Canada at the Vancouver Aquarium got there by accident. They were caught in 1967 by a group of Alaskan fishermen who were looking for salmon, not whales. The fishermen, not knowing what to do with them, offered them to the aquarium, which took them. From then on, belugas were a regular feature at the aquarium until November 2016, when the last two—Aurora, aged 30, and her calf, Quila, 21—died from what aquarium vets called an "unknown toxin." Not long after, and partly because of their deaths, the Vancouver Park Board banned the keeping and display of any more whales or dolphins in the city, effectively dealing a death blow to what had once been a common and profitable Vancouver attraction.

Today, the Vancouver Aquarium focuses its work more on education and conservation than on public entertainment. It is now run by an organization called Ocean Wise, which works to educate people about the importance of our oceans and the effects of things like climate change, overfishing, and plastic pollution. The aquarium also rescues and rehabilitates injured, sick, or orphaned marine mammals through the Marine Mammal Rescue Centre. When the animals are ready, they're usually released safely back into the wild.

Yet it wasn't that long ago that the Vancouver Aquarium exhibited not just belugas, but orcas too. Once it had as many as three. And no wonder. Until recently, the practice was a lucrative one. Aquarium owners have sold millions of tickets to people determined to see an imprisoned whale balancing a beach ball on her nose or slapping her tail like a mermaid.

But at the same time, history has taught us that keeping an orca in captivity can be full of hazards—some of them deadly. In 1989, a female orca named Kandu V attempted to attack a new orca named Corky II during a live show at SeaWorld San Diego, but wound up crashing into a wall. In 2006, another female named Kasatka repeatedly dragged a trainer named Ken Peter to the bottom of her San Diego pool after hearing her calf crying for her in another tank (luckily, he survived).

This bay on the coast of an island to the south of Iceland is where Little White and Little Grey, two belugas, now live. WDC/SEA LIFE TRUST

In 2017, she died of a bacterial infection. In 1991, a male orca name Tilikum drowned a trainer, Keltie Byrne, at a Vancouver Island aquarium called Sealand of the Pacific. Sealand closed soon after, and Tilikum was moved to SeaWorld in Florida. But tragedy struck there, too, when he killed another trainer, Dawn Brancheau, after a show in Orlando. In 2015, an eighteen-year-old female orca named Unna starved to death in San Antonio. In fact, of the estimated 165 orcas who have died in captivity around the world, 48 have perished at SeaWorld.

THE COST OF CAPTIVITY

Currently 23 orcas and 80 belugas are thought to live in 33 marine entertainment centres in North America. Because of the advent of orca and beluga breeding programs, most orcas and belugas are captive-born now. The days of capturing whales in the wild are all but over. But captive orcas, whether wild-caught or captive-born, live only a fraction of the years they would in the wild. In the wild, they can live up to 100 years (females live significantly longer than males). In captivity, they rarely live longer than fifteen. The same is true for belugas. They are now thought to live for as long as 70 years in the wild, but rarely survive more than 25 in captivity.

Because of statistics like these, there has been a growing public discomfort with the idea of keeping such intelligent animals in such tiny pools. More and more people have begun to question the ethics of keeping orcas and belugas in captivity for the mere amusement of aquarium visitors. That's why Vancouver decided to outlaw the practice. Now it's common for members of the public to protest aquariums and marine entertainment centres instead of patronizing them. Some parents have stopped taking their children to them because they believe they give kids the wrong message about how to treat such intelligent and sensitive creatures. In 2018, the Canadian government, sensing that shift, made it illegal to capture any more whales or dolphins in Canadian waters for public display. In 2019, it went a step further by banning their display altogether.

FREE WILLY

In fact, so controversial is the practice of housing what once were wild whales in tanks no bigger than swimming pools that, in 1993, a hugely popular movie called *Free Willy*

was released in cinemas across the world. It was about a young boy who goes to great lengths to rescue an orca named Willy from a marine entertainment centre. But the story turned out to be more than fiction. People soon realized there was a real "Willy" named Keiko living in an aquarium in Mexico. He had lived there for years after being captured in Iceland. A campaign was launched to rescue Keiko. It succeeded. After much negotiation and handwringing, Keiko was moved to Iceland, where he lived in a large sea pen off the Icelandic coast. The idea was to prepare him for a complete return to the wild. He remained in the pen for four years, from 1998 to 2002, after which it was decided that he was ready to be released. Unfortunately, he wasn't. Despite being a healthy whale when he was let go, he was unable to rejoin his original pod or survive on his own. He was still too dependent on humans. In 2003, he died in the wild of pneumonia.

WHALE SANCTUARIES

The idea of a whale sanctuary didn't die with Keiko, though. At the time this book was written, two twelve-year-old Icelandic beluga whales had been moved from an aquarium in Shanghai, China, where they had lived for eight years, to a holding pool on an island in south Iceland, prior to a final move to a sea sanctuary on the island's coast.

This beluga sanctuary, the first of its kind in the world, is the brainchild of two British-based marine mammal conservation organizations: SEA LIFE Trust, which also runs a seal sanctuary in the south of Britain, and Whale and Dolphin Conservation (WDC).

"If we are going to end whale and dolphin shows and the keeping of whales and dolphins in small concrete tanks for human 'entertainment,' then you have to have a solution for those creatures that are held this way," says WDC spokesman Danny Groves. "Ocean rehab and retirement sanctuaries offer that solution— an end to the shows. Those that can be released back in to the sea where they were taken from can be, and those who are unable to be released can live out the rest of their lives in peace in a much more natural sea environment where they don't have to do silly tricks for food."

The belugas, named Little Grey and Little White, made the 9,650-kilometre (6,000-mile), 11-hour flight in a specially equipped Boeing 747 in June 2019. After that, they were kept in a critical care facility, where they were examined regularly to see if they were ready for life in the "almost wild."

The sanctuary is in a 32-square-kilometre (12-square-mile) bay called Klettsvik Bay on the coast of Heimaey Island, near the southern edge of Iceland. It is bordered on all sides by natural land masses except where it opens to the sea. There, a net has been strung from one side to the other to keep the whales from escaping. But except for that, it is the "open" sea with all its charms and challenges. It's a very different environment from the one they're used to, and they had to be ready for it. After some unforeseen setbacks and delays, the whales were finally released in August 2020. Little White and Little Grey can now taste a kind of freedom they haven't enjoyed for eight years. They are finally in the sea, swimming, breaching, and feeling the sun on their backs.

The key difference between this project and the one involving Keiko is that, unlike Keiko, Little White and Little Grey will never be abandoned and expected to fare on their own. On the shore of the sanctuary is a land-based visitor and welfare centre that is continuously manned with trained welfare personnel. Not only that, the same staff can use the pontoons in the bay to gain access to the whales if they need to. Little White and Little Grey will be well looked after. They also won't be by themselves, organizers hope. Groves says the bay can accommodate up to ten whales, and SEA LIFE and

WDC are already negotiating with other aquariums about the possibility of transferring their belugas too.

Lori Marino, an American neuroscientist and behavioural biologist, dreams of a similar refuge for orcas. For years, Marino has scouted the coastlines of British Columbia, Washington State, and Nova Scotia in search of the perfect sanctuary to build a refuge at least 400 hectares (100 acres) in size for up to eight whales. Like the sanctuary in Iceland, there would also be room to build a full-service veterinary facility and education centre onshore.

She finally found such a site in February 2020 near Port Hilford on the south coast of Nova Scotia, a little more than 200 kilometres (124 miles) northeast of Halifax, and has already begun developing the property with her team.

When it's complete, she hopes that it will not only be a semi-wild home for belugas and orcas now suffering in inland concrete tanks, but that it will become a template for other similar sanctuaries. In other words, she sees it as a model for anyone else with the same passion and need to help who might want to create another whale refuge in the future. She has no completion date set for the project and still has to raise the money to build it—perhaps as much as $20 million. But dreams like these don't come cheap, and Marino is unfazed. Yes, she calls the plan "ambitious but not unrealistic." Besides, she says, she is determined because decency demands it and the whales deserve it.

Her organization's website states, "While there are sanctuaries for many land animals who are being retired from zoos and circuses, there are none yet for whales and dolphins." The establishment of the Iceland beluga sanctuary means that's no longer true, but it isn't as if more aren't needed. Marino is resolute in ensuring that that happens as soon as humanly possible.

DOLPHINS NEED SANCTUARIES, TOO

Following in the wake of Little White and Little Grey might be a pod of aquarium dolphins from Baltimore, Maryland. If everything goes according to plan, seven dolphins from the National Aquarium in Baltimore will move to a seaside sanctuary in Florida or the Caribbean, where they too will live out the rest of their lives on the edge of the Atlantic.

Dolphins have been held in captivity in North America since 1938, when the first dolphin was put on display at the Marine Studios dolphinarium in St. Augustine, Florida. The dolphin proved so popular with visitors that it wasn't long before more and more dolphins found their way into more and more aquariums in the US and Canada. Currently, there are about 475 in North America.

That's why the fate of the seven Atlantic bottlenose dolphins at the National Aquarium is so significant. If they are moved as planned, they will be the first captive dolphins in North America to be taken out of a city and placed in a lagoon on the shores of an ocean. In other words, instead of living in a world of concrete, they will, like Little Grey and Little White, live in the sea with everything the sea has to offer: fish and other marine life, seaweed, tides, and space.

At the time of writing, the aquarium still hadn't chosen a location for its sanctuary. Aquarium staff had scouted locations in Florida, Puerto Rico, and the US Virgin Islands, but they still hadn't found the ideal spot. What they want is a tropical site with fresh sea water (a place where currents continually flush debris out of the water), a naturalistic setting, and a piece of property where the aquarium can build a medical facility.

Just like the big-cat, monkey, elephant, and reptile sanctuaries you've read about so far, this dolphin sanctuary will be a place where humans will play an important role too. They'll feed the dolphins if they have to, look after their medical needs, and keep a watchful eye on them in case something goes wrong. Visitors will be allowed

It isn't enough that visitors at aquariums and marine entertainment centres can see dolphins up close; they want to see them do tricks too. JO-ANNE MCARTHUR/ WE ANIMALS

Imagine having to live your whole life in a swimming pool when nature intended for you to live in the ocean. JO-ANNE MCARTHUR/WE ANIMALS

dolphin sanctuary in 2016. Dolphins have been on display at the National Aquarium since 1990, a time when people were far less sensitive to the plight of captive marine species than they are now. But in the last twenty years, the same societal changes that forced aquariums and marine entertainment centres to rethink keeping orcas and belugas in captivity have forced dolphinariums to rethink their displays, too. The National Aquarium is the first and only such facility to consider doing something about it.

However, it's possible that in time other aquariums may follow its lead. That depends on the people who run those aquariums and whether they're prepared to do what's best for their dolphins, too. There would be room for at least twenty animals in the National Aquarium's sanctuary.

When you consider sanctuaries for wild and exotic animals, you must consider sanctuaries for whales and dolphins, too. Keiko blazed a trail when he spent four years in that Icelandic sea pen. He proved that as long as humans look after previously captive marine mammals, they can live in a contained but otherwise natural marine environment. Now Little White and Little Grey are living proof of it.

onto the site as well, but the aquarium still doesn't know how many or in what capacity. However, the sanctuary will definitely have a webcam so aquarium-goers in Baltimore can see what the sanctuary dolphins are up to day and night.

The aquarium, which attracts 1.3 million visitors a year, came up with the idea of a

FLIPPER, A TV series about a Florida park ranger, his two sons, and their pet bottle-nose dolphin, ran from 1964 to 1967 on the NBC network. Flipper was an extraordinarily intelligent dolphin who helped the family in all sorts of adventures. Whenever there was trouble, Flipper was there to lend a fin. In truth, five dolphins played Flipper—four females and a male named Clown. Clown was essential because he was the only one of the five who could balance on his tail, one of Flipper's signature stunts.

They were all trained by an employee of the Miami Seaquarium named Ric O'Barry. He became a fierce opponent of keeping whales and dolphins in captivity in 1970, after Kathy, one of the females who played Flipper, sank to the bottom of her pool and never resurfaced. She died in O'Barry's arms. He believed that Kathy, rather than living another day in captivity, had killed herself. Since then, O'Barry has dedicated his life to speaking against the harmful effects of keeping whales and dolphins in aquariums and, as a result, has become a real thorn in the aquarium industry's side.

BLACKFISH IS a 2013 documentary about the controversy around keeping whales in captivity. The film, which played in film festivals, on TV, and online, was particularly critical of SeaWorld and its record of whale injuries and deaths. SeaWorld lost millions of dollars in 2013 when people, outraged by what they saw in the movie, stopped going to SeaWorld's marine entertainment centres.

Documentaries rarely have the impact that *Blackfish* has had on the aquarium industry. Even now, the film continues to strike a chord. In fact, because of its popularity, real change has been made at SeaWorld. In 2015, the company promised to end orca shows at its park in San Diego, and in 2016, it announced it would end its orca breeding program and begin to phase out all live performances involving orcas.

If everything goes according to plan, this dolphin at the National Aquarium in Baltimore and six of his tankmates could soon be living in a seaside sanctuary once the aquarium finds the right site. SEAN LO, NATIONAL AQUARIUM

Like her fellow chimps at Chimp Haven in Louisiana, Tracy loves to be up in the tree canopy watching what's going on down below. CHIMP HAVEN

CONCLUSION
YOU CAN HELP, TOO

IT'S A STRANGE world we live in where elephants balance on circus balls, tigers exist in far greater numbers in Canada and the US than they do in India, and 4.5-metre (15-foot) pythons slither across the backs of living room sofas while young children watch TV.

No wonder there are animal sanctuaries. There have to be. Not that they're an antidote to the trade and abuse of wild or exotic animals. The only real antidote would be to change the laws that allow people to keep these animals in the first place. But for the animals who live in sanctuaries, they're a godsend. A good sanctuary will give its animals a life worth living. Good food, a safe and comfortable place to sleep, things to do, and places to roam so they don't go mad from boredom and intellectual starvation. It is an irrefutable blessing that they exist.

And there are things you can do to help them.

First and foremost, don't adopt any kind of exotic animal as a pet. No snakes. No lizards. No parrots. No monkeys. No turtles. If you keep any of these animals as a pet, it encourages the people who breed them to breed even more. The only time it's okay to adopt an exotic animal is if you get it from a rescue facility like the Greyhaven Exotic Bird Sanctuary or Parrot Island. Then you'll be saving a life. But by and large, if you want a pet, get a dog or cat. There are millions of homeless dogs and cats in shelters all over North America, and every single one of them would be grateful to live in your house. Or go to a rabbit rescue and adopt a neutered bunny. There's more to caring for a rabbit than you might realize, but they still make good pets if you learn what to do. Living with an animal can be a joy, but it has to be the right animal. And a tortoise, lizard, cockatoo, or tiger is definitely the wrong animal.

Second, don't support attractions or entertainment that feature exotic or wild animals. Happily, fewer and fewer movies use live animals (the animals you see on-screen are usually computer generated), and more and more circuses are choosing not to feature them either. The most famous about-face occurred in 2015, when the family that owns the Ringling Bros. and Barnum & Bailey Circus announced that they would no longer use elephants in their acts. But plenty of circuses still do use elephants—and tigers, lions, and leopards—so it's important to let those circuses know that you disapprove of them by not buying tickets.

Then there are marine entertainment centres, with their whales and dolphins swimming round and round—*and round*—tiny concrete pools. As you now know, there are efforts afoot to move some of these whales and dolphins to marine sanctuaries where they can experience nature again. But until all of them are released,

don't go to watch them in marine jails. Let the people who run marine entertainment centres know you're not interested in spending your money to watch misery and cruelty.

Third, if you can, make a donation to your favourite sanctuary. Not everyone is able to do this, but if you do have some spare cash (or if you decide to do some fundraising), pick a sanctuary and give it some money. Without donations, there would be no sanctuaries, and without sanctuaries, there would be no sanctuary animals.

And fourth, if there's a sanctuary near where you live, consider becoming a volunteer for it. Not only will you be doing a very good and essential deed, you'll get the chance to work with animals of a sort that you may never have seen up close before. You also may make some new friends.

You definitely can make a difference. While the things I've suggested may seem small, if 100 or 100,000 people did any combination of them, that would represent real change. You don't have to run a sanctuary to improve an animal's life. You just have to carefully consider the choices you make. The people who run animal sanctuaries are heroes of the highest order. But remember, they can only do what they do if people like you and me support them.

ACKNOWLEDGMENTS

THANK YOU TO the following people for their help in writing this book. Without their expertise, input, and most of all, their selflessness and dedication, this book and the sanctuaries it describes would not exist. They are: Lisa Wathne, Patty Finch, Kellie Heckman, Adam Roberts, Ali Crumpacker, Julie Woodyer, Ed Stewart, Lynn Cuny, Carole Baskin, Gloria Grow, Diana Goodrich, Lesley Day, Steven Ross, Casey Taylor, Jen Fierstein, Erika Fleury, Daina Liepa, Kari Bagnall, Rachel Taschenberger, Tim Ajax, Patti Ragan, Jeanna Hensler, Ken Drotar, Angela Culver, Bobbi Brink, Kate Mason, Carol Buckley, Jesse Rothacker, Robert Fearn, Jennifer Ramsey, Katie Bird, Susan Tellem, Rob Laidlaw, Val Lofvendahl, Clifford Warwick, Bree Stoddart, Janet Trumbule, Ray Parkes, Karen Windsor, Galiena Cimperman, Wesley Savoy, Lori Marino, and Danny Groves. I would also like to thank my editor, Sarah Harvey, and everyone at Heritage House for helping make this book a reality.

Foxie, who lives at the Chimpanzee Sanctuary Northwest in central Washington State, loves dolls. She is never without one. That's why donors to the sanctuary always send her new ones. CHIMPANZEE SANCTUARY NORTHWEST

BIBLIOGRAPHY

SOURCES AND FURTHER READING

Animal Finder's Guide. animalfindersguide.com.

Chan, Sewell. "SeaWorld Says It Will End Breeding of Killer Whales." *New York Times*, March 17, 2016. www.nytimes. com/2016/03/18/us/seaworld-breeding-killer-whales.html.

Exotic Animals for Sale. exoticanimalsforsale.net.

Huggins, Brittany. "Last of Big Cats Gone." *Grenada Star*, January 7, 2009. www.grenadastar.com/2009/01/07/last-of-big-cats-gone.

Lazaruk, Susan, and Glenda Luymes. "Vancouver Aquarium Bows to Pressure to Ban Whales, Dolphins." *Vancouver Sun*, January 18, 2018. vancouversun.com/news/local-news/vancouver-aquarium-bows-to-pressure-to-ban-cetaceans.

"Monkey in Coat Runs Loose at Toronto Ikea Parking Lot." *CBC News*, December 9, 2012. www.cbc.ca/news/canada/toronto/monkey-in-coat-runs-loose-at-toronto-ikea-parking-lot-1.1180677.

Muzylowski, Jodi. "Vancouver Aquarium Agrees to Cetacean Ban in New 35-year Lease Agreement." *CBC News*, June 25, 2019. www.cbc.ca/news/canada/british-columbia/vancouver-aquarium-drops-cetacean-ban-lawsuit-against-vancouver-park-board-1.5189507.

Nixon, Geoff. "The Long Goodbye of the Toronto Zoo Elephants." *CBC News*, October 12, 2013. www.cbc.ca/news/canada/toronto/the-long-goodbye-of-the-toronto-zoo-elephants-1.1894496.

Obee, Dave. "How Moby Doll Revolutionized Our Understanding of Orcas." *Times Colonist*, October 2, 2016. www.timescolonist.com/entertainment/books/how-moby-doll-revolutionized-our-understanding-of-orcas-1.2356173.

"Ontario Man Killed by Tiger He Kept on His Property." *CTV News*, January 10, 2010. www.ctvnews.ca/ontario-man-killed-by-tiger-he-kept-on-his-property-1.472255.

Rogers, S.A. "Mike Tyson's Tiger Removed from Indiana Tattoo Parlor." *Mother Nature Network*, May 29, 2010. www.mnn.com/earth-matters/animals/stories/mike-tysons-tiger-removed-from-indiana-tattoo-parlor.

Schwieg, Sarah V. "Captive Belugas Take Plane Ride to the Most Amazing

Surprise." *The Dodo*, June 20, 2019.
www.thedodo.com/in-the-wild/belugas-
little-grey-little-white-retire-sanctuary-
iceland.

SeaWorld. seaworld.com.

SANCTUARIES AND OTHER ORGANIZATIONS YOU CAN HELP

American Tortoise Rescue, California |
    tortoise.com
Big Cat Rescue, Florida | bigcatrescue.org
Born Free Foundation, UK | bornfree.org.uk
Born Free USA, Texas | bornfreeusa.org
Center for Great Apes, Florida |
    centerforgreatapes.org
Chimp Haven, Louisiana | chimphaven.org
Chimpanzee Sanctuary Northwest,
    Washington | chimpsnw.org
Chimps Inc., Oregon | chimps-inc.org
Creepy Critters Rescue, California |
    creepycrittersrescue.com
Elephant Aid International, Georgia |
    elephantaidinternational.org
Fauna Foundation, Quebec | faunafoundation.org
Forgotten Friend Reptile Sanctuary,
    Pennsylvania | forgottenfriend.org
Foster Parrots—The New England Exotic Wildlife
    Sanctuary, Rhode Island | fosterparrots.com
Global Federation of Animal Sanctuaries,
    Arizona | sanctuaryfederation.org
Greyhaven Exotic Bird Sanctuary, British
    Columbia | greyhavenbirds.com
Humane Canada | humanecanada.ca
In-Sync Exotics, Texas | insyncexotics.org
Jungle Friends Primate Sanctuary, Florida |
    junglefriends.org

Lions Tigers & Bears, California |
    lionstigersandbears.org
Marine Mammal Rescue Centre, British
    Columbia | rescue.ocean.org
Midwest Avian Adoption & Rescue Services, Inc.,
    Minnesota | maars.org
National Aquarium, Maryland | aqua.org
National Audubon Society, USA | audubon.org
Orca Aware, UK | orcaaware.org
Parrot Island Sanctuary, British Columbia |
    parrotisland.net
Performing Animal Welfare Society (PAWS),
    California | pawsweb.org
Pine Island Audubon Center, North Carolina |
    pineisland.audubon.org
Save the Chimps, Florida | savethechimps.org
SEA LIFE Trust, UK | sealifetrust.org
Story Book Farm Primate Sanctuary, Ontario |
    storybookmonkeys.org
The Elephant Sanctuary, Tennessee |
    elephants.com
The Fund for Animals, DC | fundforanimals.org
The Humane Society, DC | humanesociety.org
The Oasis Sanctuary, Arizona | the-oasis.org
The Whale Sanctuary Project, British Columbia |
    whalesanctuaryproject.org
The Wild Animal Sanctuary, Colorado |
    wildanimalsanctuary.org
The Wildcat Sanctuary, Minnesota |
    wildcatsanctuary.org
Whale and Dolphin Conservation, UK |
    uk.whales.org
Whales Online / Baleines en direct, Quebec |
    baleinesendirect.org
WildCat Ridge Sanctuary, Oregon |
    wildcatridgesanctuary.org
Zoocheck, Ontario | zoocheck.com

INDEX